Baroness Georgiana L. Bloomfield

Reminiscences of Court and Diplomatic Life

Vol. 1

Baroness Georgiana L. Bloomfield

Reminiscences of Court and Diplomatic Life
Vol. 1

ISBN/EAN: 9783337094843

Printed in Europe, USA, Canada, Australia, Japan

Cover: Foto ©Suzi / pixelio.de

More available books at **www.hansebooks.com**

COURT AND DIPLOMATIC LIFE

VOL. I.

Her Majesty the Queen.

KEGAN PAUL, TRENCH & Co.

REMINISCENCES

OF

COURT AND DIPLOMATIC LIFE

BY

GEORGIANA BARONESS BLOOMFIELD

IN TWO VOLUMES

VOL. I.

LONDON
KEGAN PAUL, TRENCH, & CO., 1 PATERNOSTER SQUARE
1883

TO THE

GRACIOUS SOVEREIGN

IN WHOSE SERVICE WERE SPENT MANY OF THE

HAPPY DAYS RECORDED IN THESE

'REMINISCENCES OF COURT AND DIPLOMATIC LIFE'

THIS WORK

IS BY PERMISSION HUMBLY DEDICATED

BY HER MAJESTY'S MOST DUTIFUL AND GRATEFUL

SERVANT AND SUBJECT

GEORGIANA BLOOMFIELD

PREFACE.

In offering this work to the public the author is influenced by no vain idea that she will thereby add to the 'History of Our Own Times;' but she believes that, just as every pawn is necessary in a game of chess, so the humblest individual fills a part on the great stage of life which no other person, however superior in talent and capacity, could fill; and therefore, had these pages not been written, the events they recall and the scenes they pourtray, truthfully though perhaps feebly, could never have been published. As nothing connected with the Court and reign of our gracious Queen can fail to interest her subjects, the author hopes her work will be received with favour and indulgence, and will interest those among her friends and relations who have a few leisure moments to devote to the perusal of these 'Reminiscences of Court and Diplomatic Life.'

G. B.

SHRIVENHAM HOUSE, BERKS:
October 13, 1882.

CONTENTS

OF

THE FIRST VOLUME.

CHAPTER I.

CHAPTER II.

CHAPTER III.

CHAPTER IV.

CHAPTER V.

CHAPTER VI.

CHAPTER VII.

CHAPTER VIII.

CHAPTER IX.

CHAPTER X.

CHAPTER XI.

ILLUSTRATIONS

TO

THE FIRST VOLUME.

REMINISCENCES.

CHAPTER I.

Birth and Parentage—Early Recollections—Ball at St. James's—Confirmation—Letters from my Mother—Her Character and Maxims—My Aunt Richmond—The Queen's Coronation—Visits to Edinburgh and Paris—Appointment as Maid of Honour.

I WAS born in London, at 51 Portland Place, on April 13, 1822, the youngest child of Thomas Henry, second Baron Ravensworth, and Maria Susannah his wife, the daughter of Mr. and Lady Ann Simpson, of Bradley Hall, co. Durham. My eldest brother Henry, afterwards first Earl of Ravensworth, and my eldest sister Maria, Marchioness of Normanby, were married before I was born; and my nephews, George Henry Constantine, Marquis of Normanby, and Henry the second Earl of Ravensworth, were both older than myself, so that I was always called the 'little auntie.' When I was about three years old my parents were disturbed one morning by a violent scuffle and altercation on the stairs leading to their room, and on inquiring the cause, 'Jack Phipps,' as he was then called, was found in tears because he said his 'little auntie' was so naughty she would not allow him to carry her upstairs.

My earliest recollections are of having heard the watchman call the hours in Portland Place, and of having a great terror of highwaymen, because my father would never travel into London after dark, for fear of the carriage being robbed. I have heard that my mother's cousin, the Earl of Strathmore, was driving one night over Finchley Common, when his carriage was stopped by two men; one went to the horses' heads, the other demanded his money or his life. Lord Strathmore, nothing daunted, stooped down and got a loaded pistol, with which he shot the robber dead; the other man then made off. Lord Strathmore drove into town, and at once gave himself up to the authorities, but it turned out that he had shot a very notorious highwayman, and he received the thanks of the community for his brave deed.

When I was four years old I was taken to a child's ball at St. James's, given by King George IV., and I distinctly remember His Majesty, who was sitting on a sofa and patted me kindly on the head; but I was greatly aggrieved because my father carried me off before supper, so I did not get my share of the beautiful bonbons which my brothers brought home. My mother used to tell me that there was a curious old schoolmistress at my father's place, Eslington in Northumberland, who planted an oak tree the day I was born, which in some mysterious manner was associated with my life. It flourished well for three years and a half, at which time its leading shoot was eaten off by some animal, and at that time I nearly succumbed to a severe attack of infantine fever. My mother, who certainly had a tinge of superstition, often said it would have made her unhappy had 'Georgie's oak' faded; but it grew and flourished for many years, and, for aught I know to the contrary, may still be growing in the park at Eslington. When I was four years old I was promoted to the schoolroom, and had a French governess. I had an excellent ear for music, and could learn a tune and beat time before I could speak. I was also extremely fond of drawing, and could always be kept quiet if I had a pencil in hand. We spent the winter of 1827 at Brighton, and Prince Paul Esterhazy, then Austrian Ambassador at the court of St. James's, dined with my father and took kind notice of me. The next morning I was taking a walk with my nursery-maid, when I espied the Prince just about to mount his horse; so I immediately ran up to him, and he received me *à bras ouverts*. Many years afterwards, when I went to Vienna as an ambassadress, the Prince recollected this incident, and treated me with the greatest kindness and cordiality.

My brothers and nephews were my only playmates, so I very soon learnt their games, and was called a 'tomboy' because I was fond of cricket, trap bat and ball, and other boyish amusements, but never cared for dolls.

I had a profusion of golden curls, of which my mother was very proud, but which I hated, and I was constantly entreating that they might be cut off, that I might have short hair like my brothers; so in an unwary moment my mother gave me leave, and no sooner was she gone out driving with my sister than I sent for the village barber and had my head shaved. Their dismay on their return home was inexpressible when in the joy of my heart I ran triumphantly to meet them, and I was greeted on all sides with indignant cries of 'Get away, you little fright, you look too hideous.'

In the year 1830 the Duke of Wellington and

Sir Walter Scott came to Ravensworth, and I can well remember the long breakfast-table, and seeing Sir Walter, but have no recollection at that time of the 'Iron Duke.'

I learnt a great number of La Fontaine's fables by heart, and my mother bought a very fine folio edition of them, which she always promised to leave me. After her death this valuable work was not to be found; in vain I claimed it and tried to find it; I was unable to do so, and my brothers declared they had never seen it. Many years had elapsed, when I happened to be dining with my sister-in-law, Mrs. Thomas Liddell. During dinner my eyes were attracted to a heap of old books which were lying pell-mell on the floor of the dining-room, and I was told they were old law books which had belonged to Mr. Ord, an uncle of my mother's, which had been sold and were to be taken away the next day. Among them I recognised my long-lost edition of La Fontaine, which I immediately claimed, to my sister-in-law's infinite surprise. The very next day it would have been removed, and I should never have recovered it.

In the year 1831 my father settled that his younger children should travel from London to Ravensworth, co. Durham, with his own horses.

The journey took nine days, and we all enjoyed it exceedingly, and visited various interesting places, among others Burghley near Stamford, and some curious Druidical stones near Boroughbridge, called the Devil's Arrows. The governess I had then was a clever woman but a very odious one, and when she left she persuaded all my family to subscribe to a work she said she was about to publish on education, in which she gave an account of us all, turning us into ridicule; and the character she gave me was that I promised to be 'an undutiful child, a turbulent wife, a despotic mother, and a tyrannical mistress.'

The next governess I had was a Swiss, who introduced the first Christmas-tree we ever saw; and I was much excited at being dressed in white muslin with a pair of goose-wings to represent the 'Enfant de Noël,' and distribute little presents to all the company assembled at Ravensworth. At that time I was alone in the schoolroom, and used to be sent out every morning to play on the terrace. I lived with the fairies, and had peopled every shrub and bush with imaginary individuals, with whom I carried on mental intercourse, so that I never missed companions of my own age, and was greatly astonished when my old aunt, Mrs. Richmond, refused to credit the stories I related about my fairy intercourse.

When I was ten years old my two brothers, George and Charles, were dangerously ill, and well do I remember my anxiety and sorrow as I watched Mr. Keat's and Sir Benjamin Brodie's carriages, when these two eminent surgeons came to visit my brothers. George arrived from Malta suffering from a spinal complaint, and was lifted out of an invalid carriage. This made a most painful impression on me. My dear brother Charles died in 1832, and his loss was my first great sorrow; but he looked so calm and beautiful, death was robbed of some of its terrors, and caused me no alarm. The next corpse I saw was that of my beautiful little niece, Caroline Barrington, who was run over in 1834 and killed on the spot. She had gone out with her brothers and sisters to see the illuminations in honour of King William IV.'s birthday. In Princes Street, Cavendish Square, the door of the carriage flew open, and Caroline fell out under the wheel. She was taken up dead, to the intense grief of her parents. She was such a very beautiful child, people in the street frequently turned round to look at her when she was out walking: her features were not the least discomposed by the accident, but remained calm and placid; her long dark eyelashes swept her cheek, and she looked after death like a sleeping angel. As she was going out she ran up to her father and asked him to kiss her. He did so, saying, 'Why, you little goose, I shall see you when you come in.' Alas! he never saw her again alive.

When I was fifteen I was confirmed in the Chapel Royal by Dr. Blomfield, Bishop of London. My mother wrote me the following letters in the previous year:—

'Percy's Cross, near Fulham, April 13, 1837.

'MY BELOVED GEORGIANA,—This day you enter into your fifteenth year, and cannot any longer be considered as a child; I shall therefore address you both as a friend as well as mother, and lay before you some considerations for the future, that I trust you will receive and lay to your heart, for they come from one who loves you only too well, but who is not blind to the faults that obscure your character. Listen to me therefore, my darling, and try to amend the failings of which I complain. God has blessed you with a naturally good disposition, and a quickness in learning; you have therefore less difficulty to encounter in your education than many young persons who, from want of memory or natural dulness, find all their lessons toil instead of pleasure. And, with all these advantages, you frequently show impatience if there is any difficulty to surmount; and not to me, but to Mademoiselle, show a spirit of contention and contradiction which is as unkind as it is disrespectful, and is in no way justified by the ready blame you are but too apt to throw upon her temper to excuse yourself. It may be true that Mademoiselle is irritable, and even unjust at times; but she is still your governess, and ought to be treated with respect. Fancy yourself, Georgiana, in her situation—far from your country, your friends and relations, with the additional evil of bad health to contend with; then think what she must suffer, and think also that the bitter cup which might be sweetened by kindness, gentleness, and forbearance on your part, is only rendered more bitter by your cold and cutting indifference, and the evident dislike you show to her society. You may (as I know you do) throw all the fault on her; but be not deceived, God is not mocked, He sees us as we are; and our Saviour has told us to take the beam from our own eyes to enable us to see clearly to take the mote from our brother's eye, therefore when you are unkind or indifferent to your governess, or haughty to your maid, or disobliging and ungracious in your manner to those persons you do not happen to like, the fault rests with you; you may try to shake off the compunctious visitings of conscience, but be assured that until you acknowledge *yourself* wrong, and determine on amendment, you will not improve. And as you are now fast approaching that period of life when you will be called upon to take upon yourself the regulation of your conduct, I am most anxious that you should for the next two years exert yourself in every way, and most of all in the government of your temper; and keep such a strict watch over yourself that neither in thought, word, nor deed shall you offend God; and that by a steady perseverance in such conduct you may present yourself to the bishop for confirmation with an inward satisfaction and peace of mind that will enable you to receive his blessing with joy and thankfulness.

'May my hopes and wishes be fulfilled, and my child prove worthy of all the love of her affectionate mother,

'M. S. R.'

'April 13, 1837.

'Bless you, my beloved child, my own dearest Georgiana, for the sweet assurances your letter contains; assurances that I am certain come from the heart, and will be kept. Oh! if you knew the depth of your mother's love, the anxious thoughts she has by day and night, and the constant prayers she puts up to the throne of grace for the happiness and welfare of her darling both in this world and the next, you would fully comprehend the comfort your dear letter has been to me, and the confidence it gives me as to your future conduct. Continue, dearest, to adhere to these good resolutions, and you will then receive the blessing of the bishop, with that holy calm and peace of mind that passeth all understanding.

'God bless you, beloved one: you will never find any one who thinks so constantly on the welfare of your soul, as well as body, as your *own* mother. So *never* forget her, even when the time of separation comes, which she trusts may be as distant as the course of nature allows.

'But we must be prepared at all times to say, "Not our will, but Thine, be done." Adieu, my dearest child.

'M. S. R.'

My confirmation produced a solemn impression upon me, although I was only examined once before it by Mr. Nelson, the incumbent of St. John's, Walham Green, Fulham; the preparation and instruction in those days being very different from what they are now, and consisting literally in the knowledge of 'the Lord's Prayer, the Ten Commandments, and the Church Catechism;' but from my earliest years my mother had impressed me with a sense of God's presence, and tried to instil religious motives into my mind. Often through life I have recalled her example and precepts. Some of the most characteristic were, 'Recollect, my dear child, that the first thing to learn is to say no to yourself;' 'Il faut savoir s'ennuyer;' and, 'Mind, you must be just before you are generous. You have no right to enjoy the luxury of giving if you owe money.' She was also fond of repeating the French dictum, 'Un homme peut braver les préjugés du monde, une femme doit s'y soumettre.' My mother was very particular about my dress, and preferred great simplicity, so that both in summer and winter I seldom wore anything but white muslin with short sleeves and coloured sashes; but she always made a great point of my being clean and tidy, and having my hair smooth and glossy. She was determined I should learn German, which I obstinately refused to do, as I disliked my governess and her language, and infinitely preferred Italian, which I thought much more sonorous and beautiful. In order to encourage me, my dear mother began learning German, though she was then past sixty, and read regularly every evening for an hour with my governess. Although she was never able to speak German fluently, she understood the language perfectly, and before she died had studied many of the best authors. She always read the Scriptures in German. Although I have known many clever and distinguished women, I have never met one more accomplished and remarkable than my mother. She painted admirably both in oils and water colours, so that her copies of the old masters are almost equal to the originals. She was very fond of music, and as a young woman played the harp and sang well. She was very well informed, read a great deal, and was always occupied. However full the house might be of guests, my mother always retired to her own sitting-room after breakfast, and occupied herself till luncheon-time, and very often till late in the afternoon, when she used to take a walk in the beautiful pleasure-grounds she laid out with so much taste at Ravensworth. Often when I came home from riding I found her, and our intimate friend Mr. Blakeney,[1] pacing

[1] Mr. John Blakeney, a brother of General Sir Edward Blakeney, was at College with my father, and accompanied my elder

up and down the terrace, till the return of the rooks warned us that it was time to go in.

My sisters all married and left home, so at thirteen I was the only daughter left; but my brother Thomas and my aunt, Mrs. Richmond, lived with us. The latter was a singular character, and many are the funny stories told of her. As a young woman she was a splendid rider; and my grandfather, who was very proud of her horsemanship, used to give her a five-pound note for jumping over a five barred gate. One day she came to a turnpike gate; but as she had forgotten her purse, the turnpike man refused to let her through, and shut the gate. In vain she told him who she was, and promised to pay on a future occasion; he positively refused to open the gate. So she backed her horse a few yards, told the groom to follow her, and took a flying leap over the gate, to the extreme astonishment and consternation of the turnpike man: she then rode off, telling him he might whistle for his money.

As a child I was very much afraid of my father, as he was very strict, and disliked the noise of children; but when I grew up he made

brothers when they went abroad. He always spent the winters at Ravensworth, and was a remarkably well-read, agreeable man, to whom I was warmly attached.

me his companion, and I was devotedly fond of him. He had a most remarkable ear for music, and modulated on the organ better than any one I ever heard. I could sit for hours listening to his playing: though he never learnt his notes, he could readily catch any melody he heard, without ever playing a false note. We all inherited my father's taste for music; and my sisters, Lady Williamson, Lady Barrington, and Lady Hardwicke, had fine voices and sang delightfully, and as girls often had the honour of singing before King George IV., who was always most kind and friendly towards my parents. It is said that one day my father was walking in Portland Place, when he met a nurse carrying a baby in her arms; and being struck by the beauty of the infant, he inquired whose it was. The nurse, much astonished, answered, 'Your own, Sir Thomas!'

When I was sixteen my mother dismissed my last governess, and I became almost the head of the house. I attended the Queen's coronation with my brother Thomas. We went to Westminster Abbey about 7 A.M., and took our places in the east transept. There we remained without moving till 5 P.M., when we descended into the body of the church, and I received some of the anointing oil, which was given away, on my pocket handkerchief. I saw the ray of sunlight shine upon our gracious Sovereign as she knelt at the communion table, which has been commemorated in Leslie's picture of the Coronation; and I also witnessed Lord Rolle's fall when he approached the throne to pay homage. In the evening we went to my sister Mrs. Trotter's house in Connaught Place, to see the fireworks in Hyde Park, which were very fine.

That autumn we visited Sir William Boothby at Ashbourne, in Derbyshire, where I had the pleasure of making the acquaintance of Mr. Charles Young, the tragedian; and we went to see Chatsworth and Haddon. I also visited the lakes in Cumberland with my mother and brother, and we paid the poet Wordsworth a pleasant visit at Ambleside.

In November my mother took me to Edinburgh, where we visited Mr. Thompson, of Duddingston, who was a very good artist. He was minister of the church at Duddingston, one of the oldest in Scotland. He took us into his studio, and painted a charming little picture for us. My brother asked him whether he was acquainted with Turner, and he answered that he knew him very well, and that he dined once at Duddingston. The room was full of pictures, but he noticed none of them; till at last he remarked, 'Mr. Thompson, there are many handsome frames, but I think I could do something better in them.' Mr. Thompson answered that he felt much flattered by Turner's making any comparison between them, as that was what he (Thompson) would never have ventured to do—a clever and gentlemanlike rebuff to Turner's rude speech. Mr. Thompson gave me a charming sketch of Craigmillar Castle; it was unfortunately lost in a ship which went down between London and Limerick in 1846.

One day my brother took me to pay a visit to Audubon, the great American ornithologist, and he took us to the Botanical Gardens. He was extremely clever and entertaining, and told us many amusing stories. We spent a couple of days at Dalmeny with Lord and Lady Rosebery, and also went to Dalkeith.

In the spring of 1839 my mother took me to Paris for a month, and we were accompanied by my brother Thomas. My mother had an old friend at Paris, Ch. Scépeaux, who lived many years in England as an *émigré* during the French Revolution, and was very intimate with my parents. He was a remarkable old man when I saw him, quite of the ancient *régime*, and must then have been past eighty. Count de Faucigny, another great Royalist, was an old friend of my brother's, and he kindly did us 'les honneurs de Paris.' We went to Versailles for the 'fête du Roi,' and I very much enjoyed seeing the beautiful gardens and 'les grandes eaux,' or all the fountains playing. The place was thronged with people, and the whole scene was very animated and amusing. I went to the Théâtre Français, where I saw Mdlle. Mars act 'Mdlle. de Belle-Isle,' one of her great parts. She was then quite an old woman; but her voice was very musical: she was graceful and most beautifully dressed, and was still very attractive: her acting was so natural and charming, I have never seen any equal to it. Although I enjoyed Paris, and only stayed there three weeks, my longing to get home again was so great, that I perfectly remember stooping down and kissing the ground when we landed at Dover, little thinking then that it would be my fate to spend the greater portion of my life abroad.

As we were travelling back to England our courier found out that Lord Bingham's carriage was in front of ours, and the rule of the road forbade our passing him. We intended sleeping at

Poix, a small place between Paris and Boulogne, and our courier was afraid we should lose the rooms, so he got a horse and rode post-haste to Poix, and arriving there just before Lord Bingham, secured the best apartment. Lord Bingham was furious, abused him in the most unmeasured terms, and was about to collar him, when he called out, 'Take care what you do, my lord, for I am an Englishman;' whereupon Lord Bingham let go his hold, and—we got our rooms.

On our return to London I was presented to the Queen, and was often invited to the small dances at Buckingham Palace, which were very select and pleasant. One lovely summer's morning we had danced till dawn, and the quadrangle being then open to the east, Her Majesty went out on the roof of the portico to see the sun rise, which was one of the most beautiful sights I ever remember. It rose behind St. Paul's, which we saw quite distinctly; Westminster Abbey and the trees in the Green Park stood out against a golden sky, and the scene remains to this day indelibly fixed on my memory. My sister, Lady Normanby, was then one of the ladies in waiting, which no doubt was the reason of my being admitted so young to court. One day the Queen expressed a desire to hear me sing, so in fear and trembling I sang one of Grisi's famous airs, but omitted a shake at the end. The Queen's quick ear immediately detected the omission, and smiling Her Majesty said, 'Does not your sister shake, Lady Normanby?' My sister immediately answered, 'Oh yes, ma'am, she is shaking all over.' The Queen, much amused, laughed heartily at the joke.

That was the year of the famous 'bedchamber row,' when, to quote the words of a recent historian, Mr. Justin McCarthy, 'Sir Robert Peel could not govern with Lady Normanby, and Lord Melbourne could not govern without her;' but the following year Sir Robert Peel came into office, and the Duchess of Sutherland and Lady Normanby resigned. The next winter my sister was staying at Ravensworth, when she received a most kind and gracious letter from the Queen, who asked whether, as a personal favour, my parents would allow me to accept the post of maid of honour. As I was the only daughter remaining at home, neither my father nor my mother liked the idea of my leaving them for three months in the year, but they were pleased and flattered by the Queen's desire that another of their daughters should be selected to wait upon Her Majesty; and referring the question to me for decision, on my expressing a decided wish to accept the offer, they waived their objections, and I was officially appointed to succeed Miss Anson, who resigned on her marriage to Sir Arthur Brooke.

Letters addressed to me by my Mother on my Appointment at Court as Maid of Honour.

Ravensworth Castle, December 2, 1841.

My own Darling Georgiana,—Having long loved you a thousand times more than myself, I have been the better able to make the sacrifice of your sweet company for one quarter in every year—a sort of preparatory ordeal to the time when I may lose you altogether should you be persuaded to quit the single state, and make some worthy man happy. Having made this sacrifice in accordance with the desires of our gracious Sovereign, and also to meet the wishes of my beloved child, I feel anxious to give some general advice as to the conduct most likely to secure your own happiness and obtain the approbation and esteem of your royal mistress during your residence at court.

In the first place, your chief study should be to please the Queen, not by base flattery or servile cringing, but by the most assiduous attention even in the merest trifles; the most rigid punctuality and obedience; not only to orders, but in being always ready at the proper time, and in the proper place.

Your natural good sense will also show you that the least brusquerie or appearance of ennui is incompatible with high breeding and the respect due to the Sovereign, and that you must accustom yourself rather to sit or stand for hours without any amusement save the resources of your own thoughts, which on such occasion will, I trust, fly to Ravensworth, and 'la povera madre,' and repeat your favourite stanzas:

> Eilende Wolken, Segler der Lüfte!
> Wer mit euch wanderte, mit euch schiffte,
> Grüsset mir freundlich mein Jugendland!

The next piece of advice I wish to impress on your mind is, that whatever you see, hear, or think, must be kept to yourself. It is almost needless to add that in whatever concerns your royal mistress your lips should be sealed; but you must likewise repulse all vain inquiries and impertinent questions, not rudely but decidedly, either by silence or pleading ignorance.

To your companions be as kind, as obliging, and as agreeable as possible, but have no confidence in any one, and avoid intimacies.

I abhor idle gossip about dress, balls, and lovers, and look upon such conversation as a positive waste of time and talents. My beloved child, keep yourself to yourself, and whatever spare time you have, employ it well, and lay not up your talents in a napkin.

Your first duty is to God; your second to your Sovereign; your third to yourself: and I do most earnestly entreat you never to retire to rest without examining truly and impartially your conduct during the day; and if your conscience acquits you of all blame, you may then lie down with an innocent and cheerful heart, and think on your absent mother; but if, on the contrary, you feel that you have left undone those things you ought to have done, or done those things you ought not to have done, you should on your knees ask pardon of your heavenly Father, and pray for strength to resist temptation in future, whether it be from vanity, extravagance, want of charity, or idleness. Dearest Georgie, be kind and benevolent to all persons under you, and so regulate your expenses as to be able to set aside a certain portion of your income exclusively for charitable purposes, and put away from you that foolish idea that to dress well you *must* wear expensive things. So far from that being so, I should say simplicity, freshness, and elegance of form constitute real perfection in a young person's dress. At the same time, though the material should not be costly, it should be *good*, and made up in the most fashionable manner; for I wish my child to be a model in dress as in everything else, and to attend particularly to her gloves and shoes, and the keeping her hair bright and glossy.

Madame de Lehzen is the lady to whom I would refer you whenever you have anything to ask for. She is (I have heard from Minnie[1]) a kind and motherly person to the young ladies; and as you are the youngest of the set, I expect she will take you under her particular protection.

I need hardly warn my modest, quiet child against intimacy or flirtation with any of the gentlemen about the court; for you cannot be too cautious where so many eyes are turned upon you, and where, under the specious garb of civility, much envy and ill-will are often concealed, and those that flatter most are least to be trusted. You have been trained up, beloved one, in the way you should go, and now are left to your own guidance; and though no one can be perfect, I have the greatest trust and confidence in your never departing from the right path: but you must

[1] The Marchioness of Normanby.

watch over yourself, and never do or say anything without *reflection*: be kind and courteous, and avoid giving pain either to equals or inferiors, and discourage in your youthful attendant anything approaching to levity, vanity, or gossiping.

The last subject on which I would say a few words is employment of time and money. The first I really can hardly wish you to change, but hope you will pursue your studies in much the same regular way, and practise music and drawing, as you have done at home. The disbursement of money is rather more difficult, as you have a larger income, and of course heavier calls and responsibilities, but as a general rule I should advise you to lay out half your salary in dress; one quarter in journeys and charities, and the remaining hundred to lay out in the funds, to form a little nest egg for any future emergency. And now, my darling child, if I have left anything unsaid that may be useful to you, you can at any time refer to me for advice, which will be readily given by your most affectionate mother; and that God may bless you, and prosper all your endeavours, shall be the constant prayer of one whose thoughts will be with her child early in the morning and late at night.

M. S. R.

CHAPTER II.

First Waiting at Windsor—Arrival of Frederick William, King of Prussia—Prince of Wales' Christening—Investiture of the Garter—Queen opened Parliament—Visited Brighton—Attempt to shoot Her Majesty—Queen's Visit to Scotland—Extracts of Letters from the Hon. Matilda Paget.

Extracts of Letters to my Mother, Lady Ravensworth.

Windsor Castle, Thursday Evening, January 20, 1842.—I arrived here about five o'clock, and was immediately shown up to my rooms, which are warm and comfortable. Shortly after, Matilda Paget, who arrived just before me, came to me and took me to Lady Lyttleton, the lady in waiting, who received me kindly. I remained some time in her room; and then, when I returned to my own, Baroness Lehzen came to me, bringing me my badge, which, as you know, is the Queen's picture, surrounded with brilliants on a red bow. I am to be presented to Her Majesty in the corridor before dinner. I have a nice sitting-room, with a pianoforte. I hear the duties are very easy, and that except at meals, or when the Queen sends for us, we may sit quietly in our rooms, which is just what I like. The Castle is being prepared for the King of Prussia's visit, and is full of workpeople. I hear they have, after much difficulty, succeeded in warming St. George's Chapel, and it is all carpeted. I found on my table two large cards of invitation to the christening and banquet. The reports of balls and festivities are untrue, though the Queen may have an impromptu dance. I already begin to feel tolerably at home, and if only I find that by constant and unceasing attention on my part, and an earnest desire to do my duty, I can succeed in satisfying my royal mistress, I dare say I shall be very happy, although my thoughts will often—very often—be at home with those I love so much better than anything else in the world.

As I am not quite sure when the post goes out, I shall write you a few lines, dearest mother, before I go to bed, to tell you that I went down-stairs with Lady Lyttleton and Miss Paget, and we waited, as is customary, in the corridor, near the door which leads to the Queen's apartment. When Her Majesty came, Lady Lyttleton presented me, and I kissed hands on my appointment as maid of honour. The Queen asked graciously after you and Minnie. We then went in to dinner; and after dinner Her Majesty talked to me for some time, asked me about my family, journey, &c., &c. The Duchess of Kent was also very kind, and desired to be remembered to you and my sisters. We were quite a small party, consisting merely of the household. In the evening the Queen and Prince Albert and some of the others played a round game, whilst, as I had asked Miss Paget to take the first waiting, I sat quietly working next Baroness Lehzen, who is very amiable to me, and Lord Charles Wellesley came and talked to us. He is odd and quaint, and amuses me. When we came up to bed Lady Lyttleton and Miss Paget both congratulated me upon the success of my first interview; and now the worst is over, and I wonder at myself at feeling so little nervous. The hours are very regular—breakfast at ten, lunch at two, dinner at eight. There is a room downstairs where we are allowed to receive our relations and friends, but they must not come upstairs.

Windsor Castle, January 21, 1842.—I have not yet seen the Queen to-day, but Her Majesty keeps very early hours, as she went to the riding-house before we breakfasted this morning. Prince Albert started for Woolwich a little after eleven to meet the King of Prussia, but it is doubtful when His Majesty will arrive to-day. I went all over the state apartments which are prepared for him. What magnificent rooms they are, and what pictures! I should like to spend all my time in studying them. Our chief duty seems to consist in giving the Queen her bouquet before dinner, which is certainly very hard work! and even this only happens every other day. I am left entirely to myself, and can employ my time as I like. The weather has been very thick and foggy ever since I left you, except the day I came up from York, which was splendid; otherwise I really should think that the sun only shines at Ravensworth.

Being the maid of honour in waiting to-day, I had to place the bouquet beside Her Majesty when she sat down to dinner, and sit next the gentleman to the Queen's right; so I was next Lord Jersey. Sarah Villiers' marriage has been postponed, because Prince Esterhazy *père* is laid up at Ratisbon with a fit of the gout. I had to play at Nainjaune, or some such game, after dinner. I did not know it the least, but soon learnt. I made some mistakes at first; but, luckily, always to my own disadvantage, which delighted Prince Albert, who is charmed whenever any one fails to claim the forfeits or prizes. I suppose I may consider myself very lucky, as I got up having won exactly threepence. We are obliged to have a supply of new shillings, sixpences, fourpences, and other penny pieces.

Windsor Castle, Saturday, January 22, 1842.—The King of Prussia has just arrived. Several messengers, at stated intervals, gave notice of his coming. We were all waiting in the corridor rather more than forty minutes. The Queen came in for a quarter of an hour. As soon as the carriage was in sight the Queen waited on the staircase, and when it arrived Her Majesty went to the door, kissed the King twice, and made him two low curtseys. I was close behind, within the doorway, and saw the meeting beautifully. It was very interesting, but soon over. The King (Frederick William IV.) is of middle size, rather fat, with an excellent countenance, and a paucity of hair. We followed the Queen to the door of her room, just at the top of the stairs, and we then retired to our rooms till dinner. Rather a curious coincidence happened just now in the corridor. Whilst we were waiting for the Queen, Lord Charles Wellesley was sitting under a large picture, and I laughingly told him to take care it did not come down on his head.

He said, 'No danger;' when, scarcely five minutes after, a large portrait of the Duke of Kent came thundering down from over the very door through which the Queen and Prince always pass. Luckily, no mischief was done; but it was rather curious, and I am called a witch! The Queen introduced me herself to the King of Prussia, after dinner yesterday. Most of the unfortunate Germans were prevented coming down last night owing to the non-arrival of their luggage; but I have made their acquaintance to-day. They are all oldish men; their names are Count Stolberg, General Neumann, Colonel von Brauhitch, A.D.C., M. de Meyering, and Baron Humboldt.

Lord Hardwicke, who is the lord in waiting appointed to attend upon the King, told them that I speak German, which of course they prefer. You never heard of anything so unlucky as Lord Hardwicke's voyage. He was to command the squadron which was to bring the King of Prussia over to England, and was to have started on Tuesday, on board the 'Firebrand,' when, just as they got the steam up, the boiler burst; so they had to wait till that was repaired. They started at night, and went aground, but got off without damage. The fog was so thick on the river, the other steamer belonging to the squadron ran against the 'Firebrand,' and broke its figure-head. The third steamer ran ashore without the possibility of moving. The pilots refused to continue the passage, saying it was not safe; but Lord Hardwicke, with his usual determination, said he would take the responsibility upon himself, and insisted upon going on to the Nore, as he did not consider there was any danger. They accordingly reached it in safety, and were ready to cross to Ostend at daybreak the next morning.

The other two frigates were prevented from crossing the Channel, and the second steamer broke her paddles; so the 'Firebrand' steamed alone into Ostend Harbour, and arrived just as the King of Prussia drove up to the palace. His Majesty would not sail that evening, so Lord Hardwicke dined with the King of the Belgians, and returned to his ship for the night. But his troubles were not over; for he had scarcely got to bed when the Queen's cook walked into the sea, and was nearly drowned. Lord Hardwicke rushed on deck in his shirt, and called so loud that another steamer sent off a boat. In the meantime, one of the sailors slipped down the ladder, and got hold of the cook. He held him for some time, and then said he could do so no longer; but Lord Hardwicke encouraged him, and threw out a rope, asking at the same time whether he had got the cook. The sailor replied he had his head tight between his knees, which, as the water was up to the sailor's neck, was a useful way of saving a drowning man. Luckily at that moment the boat came up, and they were hauled up on deck, the cook being to all appearance quite dead. They, however, put him into warm blankets, pumped the water up, and rubbed him, and in about half an hour the man began to shake himself, and soon recovered; but Lord Hardwicke, who in the excitement of the moment never thought of himself, caught a bad cold from standing so long in his shirt. However, he was very thankful to have been instrumental in saving a fellow-creature's life.

I cannot tell you how kind the Duchess of Buccleuch (the Mistress of the Robes) is to me. Divine service was performed in the Castle this morning; Dr. Blomfield, Bishop of London, preached a beautiful sermon from John iii. 8. He impressed upon us the importance of the sacrament of baptism as the appointed means whereby we are admitted members of the Church of Christ on earth, which, we hope, will make us members of it hereafter in heaven. He alluded to the interesting event which is to take place on Tuesday (the Prince of Wales' christening).

I had a very amusing evening yesterday. Colonel von Brauhitch made me laugh, for he begged to know when he might be allowed to pay his respects to me; so I told him we are not allowed to receive visitors in our rooms, and that even when my own brother comes I have to receive him in the waiting-room downstairs. This seemed perfectly incomprehensible to my German friend, who insisted upon it that I made a mistake, and did not know the rules; so he went off to Madame de Lehzen, who of course told him exactly what I had said; upon which he came back to me, and bemoaned the tyranny which is exercised over us.[1] The Castle will be quite full to-day and to-morrow, and we have been obliged to give up our rooms for two days. We have got rooms higher up, which are warm and comfortable, so I do not mind.

Windsor Castle, January 25, 1842.—The christening took place exactly at one o'clock, and it was a beautiful sight. The sponsors were the

[1] He was a young-looking man, and although a grandfather he was a great flirt, and amused himself by making up to me; so he was extremel indignant one day when old General Neumann came up to him and said, 'Mais, mon cher, souvenez-vous donc que vous êtes grand-père!'

King of Prussia, the Duke of Cambridge, and Prince Ferdinand of Saxe-Coburg; the Duchess of Kent, the Duchess of Cambridge, and Princess Augusta. They stood on the right side of the communion table; the Queen, Prince Albert, the infant Prince, the rest of the Royal Family and the court on the left side, Her Majesty being nearly in the centre. I was just behind the Duchess of Buccleuch. The Archbishop of Canterbury read the service, and performed it very well, though he appeared very nervous. The Prince of Wales is a beautiful baby, with fine large eyes, and is as lively and intelligent-looking as most children of six or eight months. The Duchess of Buccleuch took him from the nurse and put him into the Archbishop's arms, which she did gracefully and well. After the ceremony the choir sang the Hallelujah Chorus, which was very thrilling. The installation of the Garter took place as soon as we returned to the Castle. Only the Mistress of the Robes and the lady in waiting were in actual attendance on the Queen; but we remained in the next room, and as the doors were open we saw the whole ceremony. The oath is very fine, and the King of Prussia seemed much impressed by it, and clasped his hands fervently as if he felt every word. After the Queen had buckled on the Garter and given the ribbon, His Majesty shook hands all round with the knights, and then the ceremony concluded

I saw and shook hands with the Duke of Wellington, Sir Robert Peel, the Duke of Rutland, &c., &c. The Duke is looking well, and stood behind the Queen during the christening, bearing the great sword of state. I have been sitting all the afternoon with the Duchess of Northumberland, who was, as usual, cheerful and amiable. She gave me a beautiful bouquet, which I immediately took to the Duchess of Buccleuch, who was delighted with it. The banquet last night was quite magnificent, and so well managed that every one was served as perfectly as if there had only been the usual number at dinner. The table reached from one end of St. George's Hall to the other, and was literally covered with gold plate and thousands of wax candles. I do not know how many sat down. I was very lucky, as I sat next Lord Hardwicke. He has so much to do that of course I see but little of him, so we were both glad of an opportunity of sitting next each other. The *coup d'œil* from the galleries in the hall must have been very fine. There was music in the evening in the Waterloo Gallery; and an immense gold vessel, more like a bath than anything else, containing thirty dozen of wine, was filled with mulled claret, to the no small surprise of the Prussians, who thought, I believe, that another royal duke was to be drowned in mulled claret instead of Malmsey! The weather yesterday was brilliant, with a bright sun, and the chapel was not at all cold.

Windsor Castle, January 28, 1842.—The Duke of Wellington came here on Monday, and I had the great pleasure and honour of going in to dinner with him on Wednesday, and sitting next Sir Robert Peel. Lady Jersey and Clementina came yesterday. Sarah is to be married on Saturday week. We have had most lovely weather, and no snow; it was quite hot for walking to-day.

Windsor Castle, January 29, 1842.—There was a little dance last night for young Prince Leopold of Saxe-Coburg's amusement. There were only just enough ladies to make up a quadrille. The Queen danced the first with the King of Prussia. Although he is rather stout, he danced very well and gracefully. We finished with a country dance, with every sort of strange figure. I think the Queen must have been studying some old books, and concentrated the figures of several centuries into this one country dance.

The Duke of Wellington remarked to me that he saw a great likeness between the King and George IV., and he has the same kind, gracious manner. I sat next Lord Stanley at breakfast yesterday; he was very funny and amusing, and remarked what a great political change would have taken place if all Her Majesty's Ministers had been smashed *en masse* when they came down together by rail the other day; and he added he thought it would be a very fair trial, in case of an equal division, if the leaders of each party were to get on two engines and have a collision.

Buckingham Palace, February 4, 1842.—The King of Prussia is just gone, and we all feel quite melancholy at his departure. We got so accustomed to seeing His Majesty and his suite, and they were all so amiable and enjoyed their visit so much, that it was quite touching to bid them farewell. The Queen breakfasted with His Majesty, and when he went away she accompanied him to the door and kissed his cheek; after which she made him a low curtsey, and waited till the carriage drove off. I should say from all accounts that the visit has gone off as well as possible. The King has done more in a short time than any one ever did before. The Prussians were very much struck yesterday at the opening of Parliament, and it was a very interesting sight. I went with Lady Jolliffe, Miss Paget, and Lady Fanny Howard. We sat in the gallery immediately opposite the door to the right of the throne, saw the Queen enter, and heard every word of the speech. Her Majesty looked rather pale, but her manner on all these occasions is quite perfect, full of grace and dignity, and her voice was firm and as clear as a silver bell. It is quite remarkable how well the Queen reads. It was so pretty to see her after she had finished, for she stopped after descending from the throne, turned to the King of Prussia, and made him a low curtsey. The House was very full, and I saw quantities of acquaintances, but had no opportunity of speaking to any one. Miss Stuart (afterwards Marchioness of Waterford) was there, looking strikingly handsome. She wore a turquoise-blue velvet, which was very becoming, and she was like one of the Madonnas she is so fond of painting. The Queen's speech was rather a long one, but contained more matter than usual. Her Majesty is very well, and did not seem at all fatigued in the evening, though I think she was rather nervous, and the House of Commons kept her such a long time waiting. Lady Jocelyn has succeeded

Lady Lyttelton in waiting. On the day of the christening, when all was over, Lady Lyttelton expressed her hope that the King of Prussia was not fatigued; upon which he answered, 'Comment donc fatigué, depuis mon arrivée en Angleterre je n'éprouve que joie, joie, joie, et toujours joie, que Dieu bénisse l'enfant!' At the Archbishop of Canterbury's he gave us the toast 'The Queen and the Church, for they can *never* be separated.' Yesterday, when Lord De la Warr (the Lord Chamberlain) and the different attendants were backing and bowing in taking His Majesty to the carriage, he said, 'De grâce ne faites donc pas cette cérémonie pour moi, allez vous en, allez vous en!'

We are to go to Brighton next Tuesday. I did not get out to-day, as I was in waiting, and had to receive the dear old Duchess of Gloucester, who came to see the Queen. Lady Georgiana Bathurst told me she thought she had been doing a little too much lately, as Her Royal Highness would go to the Duke of Sutherland's, the Duke of Wellington's, and a party at Cambridge House; besides an early luncheon at the Duke of Sussex's, where the King of Prussia made a very pretty speech. I hear he was so affected when he went on board after the review yesterday that he wept.

Windsor Castle, February 9, 1842.—We went to St. George's this morning, and after the service I went to look at the monument of the Princess Charlotte. Parts of it are beautiful, but too much gilt. I like the figures of the mourners around the body the most, and their deep distress is well represented. What a beautiful chapel St. George's is! but I never can understand why the royal closets in all the churches are the worst places for seeing and hearing. The royal closet at St. George's is so disagreeable, I always go into the choir whenever I can. Miss Cavendish came to dinner last night, after attending the Esterhazy-Villiers marriage, which took place first at Chandos House, according to the Roman Catholic form, and then at St. George's, Hanover Square. Poor old Lord Jersey was so unhappy, he did not attempt to restrain his tears, which flowed abundantly.

The Pavilion, Brighton, February 10, 1842.—We left Windsor a little after eight, and arrived here at twenty minutes before three. The roads were very heavy, but the Queen always travels with relays of her own horses, so we came a capital pace. We stopped at Reigate, and there I had a good opportunity of seeing the two children. The Princess Royal is very pretty, and the Prince of Wales is such a very fine baby. Crowds of people assembled, and we had to go a foot's pace from the entrance of the town; the windows and balconies were all filled with people waving and cheering, and a great many gentlemen came and met us a long way off, and joined the escort; the road for four miles was lined with carriages. The Queen has not been here since her marriage, so I dare say it will amuse Her Majesty to show this place to Prince Albert. Our rooms are tolerably comfortable, but Lady Jocelyn's, where I am sitting, smokes so abominably I am nearly suffocated. We have just heard that Prince Albert's brother, Prince Ernest of Saxe-Coburg, is engaged to be married to the Princess Alexandrina of Baden.

I have been walking in the Pavilion garden, which is odious; so low and damp, without a glimpse of the 'deep and dark blue ocean;' one might as well pace round and round Berkeley Square. I suppose it *is* sea air, but so mixed with soot and smoke it loses half its value. Lady Jocelyn was as glad as I was to get out this morning, and made me laugh, saying she felt like a bird in a cage, so exactly my own sensations. There were great rejoicings and illuminations, fireworks, &c., here last night, which were rather pretty, but not sent off quickly enough. The rooms here are certainly very striking at night, and unlike every other palace. I was interested at hearing Lord Jocelyn, who had lately returned from China, say that it was a perfect specimen of a Chinese house. The music room, with its dome covered with silver scales, was very fairy-like when lighted up in the evening, and a beautiful room for music. I believe that one room alone cost 80,000*l.*, and the whole place was a strange specimen of royal eccentricity, and a most uncomfortable, dull residence, so I never wondered at the Queen's getting rid of it. Her Majesty could not move out without being mobbed, and there was neither privacy nor pleasure to be had there.

I remember going one day to call on Lady Shannon, who told me that the Sunday before at church her little son remarked that he supposed that Sunday was called *Queen*quagesima after the Queen!

Pavilion, Brighton, February 12, 1842.—The weather to-day is beautiful, there is not a cloud in the sky, and the sea is deep blue. I never felt anything more balmy and delicious than the air on the pier, and I constantly sit with my window wide open. The crocus and snowdrops are out in the garden, besides several bits of fresh green, which give quite an appearance of spring. We went yesterday with the Queen to the chapel belonging to the Pavilion, and Mr. James Anderson preached. In the afternoon I went and heard his brother, Mr. Robert Anderson, who preaches extempore, and gave an excellent and uncommon sermon. He has great command of language and remarkable facility. Lady Jocelyn goes out of waiting tomorrow, which I regret. She is going back to Ireland immediately, as Lord Jocelyn is High Sheriff this year. I leave this early on Thursday. (Thus terminated my first waiting.)

On May 29 I was in waiting at Buckingham Palace, and had attended divine service on Sunday at the Chapel Royal with the Queen and Prince Albert. As we were driving back from church there was a momentary delay in the Birdcage Walk, but the ladies in waiting, who were in a second carriage, knew not the cause of the stoppage, but when we reached Buckingham Palace we noticed that the Prince looked annoyed and went away with the equerries. The Queen, who was quite calm and collected, walked up the grand staircase to her apartments, talking to her ladies, and spoke of the sermon which had been preached by Dr. Blomfield, the Bishop of London. Her Majesty showed no signs of nervousness, and dismissed us as usual. The following day the lady in waiting did not appear at luncheon, so my companion maid of honour, Matilda Paget, and I waited at home all the afternoon, expecting a summons to drive with the Queen, who was in the habit of taking us when she did not take the lady in waiting. It was my day out of waiting, and I had been particularly anxious to go home to see my mother, who was not very well, so I was not a little disappointed when, about six o'clock, we saw the Queen drive off in an open carriage with Prince Albert. I remarked that it was very hard to keep us in the whole afternoon when we were not wanted, and I went off grumbling to take a walk in the Palace gardens. I was much horrified to learn on my return that the Queen had been shot at by a lad of the name of Francis. That evening the Queen was talking to Sir Robert Peel, who was then Prime Minister, and who was much affected at the risk Her Majesty had run, when the Queen turned to me and said, 'I dare say, Georgy, you were surprised at not driving with me this afternoon, but the fact was that as we returned from church yesterday a man presented a pistol at the carriage window which flashed in the pan; we were so taken by surprise that he had time to escape, so I knew what was hanging over me, and was determined to expose no life but my own.' Her Majesty added, the report had been less loud than it was when Oxford fired at her, and that indeed she should not have noticed it had she not been expecting it the whole time she was driving. This was a noble instance of the Queen's courage and kind consideration for others, for certainly the assassin might have been more bewildered by seeing three ladies drive rapidly by than when he saw Her Majesty sitting alone by her husband.[1]

Extract from a Letter of the Hon. Matilda Paget.

'*Taymouth Castle, September* 9, 1842.—I must write to-night, as the post goes out at half-past six A.M., which I think you will say is peculiar! There is an immense party here. Roxburghs, Kinnouls, Abercorns, Buccleuchs, Belhavens, Duchess of Sutherland and her eldest daughter, Lady Elizabeth, who is charming. Lord Lorne, Lord Mansfield, Lord Lauderdale and his brothers, Sir John and Lady Elizabeth Pringle and their two daughters, besides many others. I wish I

[1] See *Life of the Prince Consort*, vol. ii. p. 139.

could give you a faint notion of the beauty and magnificence of this place, but it is far beyond anything *I* ever saw before. The Queen's arrival on Wednesday was, without any exception, the most glorious sight I ever beheld. This splendid castle, surrounded by the most beautiful scenery, and thousands of kilted Highlanders in every direction. The weather was bright and fine, bands and bagpipes playing, every one cheering, and in the evening there were the most lovely illuminations and fireworks, and the Highlanders danced reels. We lunched at Dunkeld, Lord Glenlyon's, on our way here, and I can never forget the reception by Lord Glenlyon and his whole clan. The Queen walked down the ranks of the Highlanders, and the cheering was deafening. We lunched in a tent, and the Highlanders marched up and down with drawn swords, and then danced the sword dance. Lord James Murray, Lord Glenlyon's brother, danced it very beautifully. The only thing that marred one's pleasure was poor Lord Glenlyon himself, who is quite young but quite blind, and it was so touching to see him in his beautiful kilt going about doing the honours, but unable to see anything, his wife *almost* leading him about.

'Here it is as though one were living centuries ago! it is all so picturesque and interesting.

'From the windows one sees lovely mountains, and down below Highlanders walking up and down with drawn swords and shields, and there is an encampment of tents for the men. Yesterday we took the most lovely drive, and I longed for your pencil—what sketches you would have made! lakes, mountains, and trees, and then a Highlander appearing as if by magic in some beautiful wild path. I am quite enchanted with it all.

'The Prince was out shooting all the morning, and had capital sport, killing eighteen roes, besides quantities of grouse; and then there was a regular Highland scene. All the animals were brought up to the house, and carried between two foresters in such pretty dresses; the gentlemen wore kilts. To-night there is to be a ball here. There are to be two bands, a quadrille band and a Scotch one, for reels, &c. To-morrow we go to Drummond Castle, thirty miles from hence. We travelled all day with Lord Aberdeen and Sir Robert Peel, and I had such a nice interview with the dear Queen this morning. I have had to write to Baroness Lehzen daily, and

I think we shall start for England on Thursday, the 15th; but I know nothing positively yet.

'Lady Abercorn is so charming, and Lady Breadalbane looks lovely, but *dead*. I never saw any one alive look as she does. Last night Mr. Wilson sang some Scotch songs. I think I liked Scone less than the rest of our expedition. It was very fine, but so sombre, dull, and cold; but I liked Lord Mansfield very much.'

CHAPTER III.

Interview with the Royal Children—Royal Kitchen and Plate—Amusing Breakfast at Windsor with Lord Stanley and Sir Robert Peel—Bowood—Rides with the Queen at Windsor—The Duke of Wellington and the Princess Royal—Dinner at Frogmore.

Windsor Castle, December 22, 1842.—I arrived yesterday, but did not see the Queen till just before dinner, when we received Her Majesty in the corridor. She kissed us both, and as I was in waiting, I sat within one of the Queen at dinner, and next Lord Ormond. Her Majesty made many inquiries after you, papa, and all my family, and expressed regret at hearing that papa had been unwell. After dinner I delivered the Duchess of Gloucester's present and letter; and when the gentlemen came in, Prince Albert asked me about the festivities at Ravensworth on the coming of age of my eldest brother's son Henry, and whether I had been practising much, and whether we had been a very large family party. Both he and the Queen laughed when I told them we were eighteen brothers and sisters, including the married ones; and as usual the Queen joked about the number of my nephews and nieces. I am so pleased at the smallness of the party here, as I always think Court so much pleasanter without guests, as we see so much more of the dear Queen.

Windsor Castle, December 26, 1842.—I had a most satisfactory interview on Saturday with the royal children and Lady Lyttelton. Lady Canning, Miss Lister, and I went to her room, and then she took us down to the nursery. The children (the Princess Royal and Prince of Wales) are both much grown and improved. The Princess Royal is a darling; she was in immense spirits, and showed off to great advantage. She runs about now, talks at any rate, and was delighted with two new frocks the Duchess of Kent had sent her as a Christmas-box. She took first one and then the other, and showed them to each of us; and then she desired me to put one on, which was not as practicable as I could have wished; but I held it up for her, to her great delight. She is very fat, and was dressed in a dark blue velvet frock, with little white shoes, muslin sleeves gathered tight to her arm, and yellow kid mittens. The Prince of Wales has had a cold, but he is a dear little boy ; and considering we were all strangers, I never saw such good children, and they were not a bit shy. The Prince has large eyes, curly hair, and is a little like the child in your copy of the 'Marriage of St. Catherine.' The Queen sent for us and Lady Canning at five o'clock on Saturday, and gave us each a Christmas-box. Mine is a brooch of dark blue and light blue enamel, with two rubies and a diamond in the shape of a bow. Miss Lister has a brooch something similar, and Lady Canning the bracelet always given to the Ladies of the Bedchamber, with a portrait of the Queen from Winterhalter's picture. The Queen also gave Lady Canning a nice Paisley shawl, and before dinner all the household received presents—pins, studs, rings, &c., &c. After dinner there were three lovely Christmas-trees, and there was some very pretty music in the evening. The Queen gave me leave of absence from chapel yesterday morning, so I went to St. George's with Lady Lyttelton. There was the beautiful anthem of 'There were shepherds,' and also the 'Glory to God :' a boy of the name of Forster has a lovely voice, and yesterday he surpassed himself.

Windsor Castle, December 31, 1842.—The last day of the year! I always feel sorry when that comes; it feels like parting from an old friend. And there is something particularly solemn to me in the thought that another year, with all its joys and sorrows, has passed away, never to return. However, I sincerely trust the new year will bring happiness to all, but especially to you and my dear father. I wish you both many, many happy returns of the day; and may it please the all-wise and bountiful Giver of every blessing long to spare your precious lives, which not only make the chief happiness of your children, but that of all around you. God bless you both.

When I came home from driving with Lady Canning yesterday, we were told that Her Majesty and the Prince were going to have a conjugal *tête-à-tête* dinner, and did not mean to appear. So the household dined together in the Oak Room, and I thought the evening remarkably long and dull, as when I am in waiting it seems hard not to see the Queen at least once a day.

This evening Charles Murray (Controller of the Household) took us over the plate and china rooms, and the kitchen. They are really most magnificent and interesting. I could scarcely have imagined such a display of gold plate, which is by far the largest collection in the world, and is valued, I am told, at above two millions sterling. Some of the cups executed by Benvenuto Cellini are lovely. I think I admired some of the china even more than the plate, especially one service of Sèvres and one of old Chelsea. The kitchen was a curious sight enough; and I could not help reflecting how little I thought, in eating my simple dinner every day, of the preparation and expense which attends what comes as a matter of course. The fire was more like Nebuchadnezzar's 'burning fiery furnace' than anything else I can think of; and though there is now no company at Windsor, there were at least fifteen or twenty large joints of meat roasting. Charles Murray told me that last year they fed at dinner a hundred and thirteen thousand people. It sounds perfectly incredible; but every day a correct list is kept of the number of mouths fed; and this does not include the ball suppers, &c., &c., but merely dinners.

The Queen desired Charles Murray to write to the Bishop of Salisbury for the solution of the detestable riddle which was sent here, and said to have been written by him. He answers that the whole thing is perfectly untrue and unfounded; that he never wrote it, or offered any reward for its explanation, and he believes the whole thing to be a hoax. I expect the Queen will be very angry, as both Her Majesty and the Prince have been puzzling their brains for four days with it. The weather is lovely, like spring, with a soft westerly wind.

Windsor Castle, January 4, 1843.—The Normanbys arrived here yesterday, and are in great spirits. We had such a very agreeable breakfast this morning. Sir Robert Peel had despatched a messenger to summon the Ministers to a Council to-day, and he said if they could not muster enough, he must call in Normanby, which made us all laugh, and of course caused many jokes. Lord Stanley (afterwards the Earl of Derby) said that a second edition of the *Globe* would be published with an article headed 'Extraordinary Schism in the Government; Coalition; Lord Normanby sent for; Council held at Windsor without the knowledge of some of the Ministers, &c., &c.;' and a little private paragraph to the effect that 'it was worthy of remark that Viscountess Canning had gone out of waiting yesterday.' Altogether it was very amusing, and the banter passed off with great fun and good nature on all sides.

The Queen having gone to Claremont for a few days, during which time my services were not required, gave me leave to accompany my sister, Lady Barrington, on a visit to Lord and Lady Lansdowne at Bowood.

Bowood, January 8, 1843.—I came here yesterday with the Barringtons, and we were most kindly received by Lord and Lady Lansdowne. The party in the house consists of Lady Kerry, Lord Bathurst and his brother William, Lord Shelburne, the Lionel Rothschilds, Mr. James Howard (Lord Suffolk's son), Mr. Smith (a brother of Sidney Smith's), and Miss Fox. We had a great deal of music last night, and I sang several duets with Janey (Viscountess Barrington). The house is thoroughly comfortable, and contains some beautiful pictures, ancient and modern. It is rather a curiously-shaped mansion, as it has been added to at different times without regard to the original plan. There is no magnificence, but the rooms are in good proportion and very well furnished, the pictures admirably lighted. Those in the dining-room are by Stanfield and Eastlake. There is a beautiful Murillo in the drawing-room and a Sir Joshua of Mrs. Sheridan—a lovely picture. The pleasure-grounds are very pretty. I never saw finer specimens of hemlock spruce, cedars, cypress, red cedars, and ivy. We went this morning to a church built by Lord Lansdowne, and there was afternoon service, and a sermon in the private chapel, which is connected with the house by the conservatory. I like Lady Lansdowne very much. She seems so excellent and amiable, and is most good-natured to me. It is very melancholy to see Lady Kerry and Lord Shelburne, the one having lost her husband, the other his wife, so early. Last night we looked over two drawers full of drawings by the old masters: some of them are very fine; and I think I almost prefer an original sketch to a finished picture, as it is so interesting to see the artist's first impressions, and sketches are often so spirited. There are one or two Vandykes, a Poussin, and a Raphael, and such quantities of *objets d'art* in every corner of the house that one sees something fresh to admire every hour. I have been copying a lovely sketch of the Madonna del Sacco by Andrea del Sarto, and we walked round the gardens and pleasure-grounds. I admired a beautiful Cape jessamine, which is a great rarity at this season of the year; so Lady Lansdowne picked it and gave it to me, saying she was anxious to make the place as pleasant to me as possible in order to tempt me to return, which is scarcely necessary, as I never enjoyed a visit more in my life, and shall be very sorry to leave this charming hospitable roof. Tommy Moore came here yesterday, and I was delighted to have an opportunity of seeing and hearing him. His voice is weak now, and he shuts the pianoforte up when he accompanies himself; but his enunciation is wonderful, and he sings with so much spirit, I admire his singing very much. He sang several of my old favourites, but I could not prevail upon him to sing 'I saw from the beach,' which I wanted to hear. He is a very small man, with curly hair and sharp bright eyes. I have just received a kind note from the Duchess of Norfolk, who is in waiting at Claremont, to say I need not return to Windsor before Monday. She adds, 'Archdeacon Wilberforce declared yesterday that he could tell people's characters by their writing. I think *you* would come off very well with him.'

Bowood, January 12, 1843.—We went to a ball given by Mr. and Mrs. Heneage about five miles from here. The house was built in James's time, and is very pretty, with a beautiful staircase and two galleries. I confess I felt very much like Jack the Giant-killer when he went up the bean-stalk into the unknown country, but I found several acquaintances and danced a great deal, but we came away early, and I need not say I was very glad to get back.

We left Bowood on the 14th, with great regret;

as I had been unable to finish the sketch I began of the Madonna del Sacco, Lord Lansdowne most kindly insisted upon bringing the picture to London for me, and the following spring I got a note from him to say he hoped I would call at Lansdowne House and fetch it, as he should be much disappointed if I refused to do so. I accordingly took it home, and prized it as the apple of my eye. The day when I was putting the finishing stroke to the copy I made in water colours, my mother sent to ask for some papers she wanted which I had put in the drawer of my escritoire. In pulling it out rather in a hurry, it tipped over the easel on which the precious picture was placed, and it fell forward on a china mug, to my intense grief and consternation. When I lifted it up I saw that a round bit had been scraped clean off the sky, but the picture being painted on panel was not otherwise injured. I was greatly distressed, and when I went down to tell my mother what had occurred she was quite frightened at my paleness, and said I looked as if I had seen a ghost. I asked what I must do; so she said, 'Of course there is but one thing to do: you must write at once and tell Lord Lansdowne what has occurred.' This I did in fear and trembling, when I got the kindest, most courteous answer from him to beg me not to distress myself, and declining even to look at the picture till my brother Thomas, who was an excellent artist, had it repaired. This of course was a great relief to my mind, but I made a vow, which I have religiously kept ever since, never to borrow a valuable work of art again.

Windsor Castle, August 4, 1843.—I went to-day at twelve to pay Madame Angelat a visit in her room, the lady in waiting to Princess Clementine, and she gave me many interesting details of the death of the Duc d'Orléans. She has lived twenty-three years with Princess Clementine, was with her at the time of that melancholy catastrophe, and accompanied her and the Duchesse de Nemours when they went to meet the poor Duchesse d'Orléans on her road to Paris. The misery of the Queen Marie Amélie was something too painful; and though now she is resigned, and at times even cheerful, the chief delight of her life is gone, and she will never be really happy again; for she perfectly adored her son, and he was equally devoted to her. After the accident happened she knelt over the body, crying in accents of the deepest despair, 'Mon Dieu, mon Dieu, prenez ma vie, mais sauvez mon fils.' I heard many other interesting particulars which I cannot write, but altogether it must have been a most terrible time. After luncheon I went with Madame Angelat and the Duchess of Oldenburg's lady in waiting to St. George's Hall and the state apartments, and since then have been driving, so farewell.

Windsor Castle, August 10, 1843.—The Queen returned here at two o'clock yesterday, and you will see by the papers what a large party we were at dinner. I never felt anything so delicious as the night yesterday; it was so hot that we all went out without any extra wraps, and the Queen walked round the terrace, followed by her suite and guests. The moon was so brilliant, I could have fancied myself in Italy; and the whole scene was most picturesque and like a scene on the stage, the Castle lighted up in the background, and all the company in their evening dresses, Windsor uniforms, &c., &c. I was quite sorry to come in. The Prince walked with the Duke of Wellington, and I was amused at hearing a long description about . . . larders; it might have been a French cook instead of the great hero of Waterloo.

Windsor Castle, August 12.—I had a delightful ride with the Queen yesterday, who most kindly lent me her habit, hat, collar, and cuffs. Considering the great difference in our figures, the habit fitted me wonderfully. I just pinned it over in front, and presented quite a respectable figure. Curiously enough, I rode Zarifa, a grey mare which once belonged to Susie (my sister the Countess of Hardwicke). Is it not a singular coincidence that the first time I rode here I should have her old horse? but it is a particularly nice one, and very quiet, with an excellent mouth and safe action, and easy enough for me, though the Queen rather complained of her being rough. We rode all about the park for two hours and a quarter, and I never enjoyed anything more. The evening was delicious, and the lights and shades among the fine old oaks and ferns *so* beautiful. I do hope the Queen will continue to ride, because as neither Lady Dunmore nor Matilda Paget ever do, I should probably always have to accompany Her Majesty. Riding always agrees with me, and this park is so perfect. No one dined here last night, so we talked a great deal to the Queen, and afterwards played at vingt-et-un, and I won eightpence, which was much for me, as I generally come off second best at the round games. The Queen told us a funny anecdote of the little Princess

Royal. Whilst they were driving the other day the Queen called her, as she often does, 'Missy.' The Princess took no notice the first time, but the next she looked up very indignantly, and said to her mother, 'I'm not Missy, I'm the Princess Royal.' She speaks French fluently, and she was reading the other day, when Lady Lyttelton went up to her; so she motioned her away with her hand, and said, 'N'approchez pas moi, moi ne veut pas vous.'

Windsor Castle, August 11.—The Duchess of Kent very kindly sent me an immense heap of music yesterday, vocal and instrumental. I delight in looking over new music. We took a long drive, and the more I see of this lovely park the more I admire it; the scenery varies so much, that almost every day I become acquainted with fresh beauties. The Queen went with the little Princess and the Duchess of Buccleuch in one of the small pony carriages, and before we started there was a little delay, so I witnessed a most interesting scene between the Duke of Wellington and the Princess. She looked at him very hard, and he bent down in the most gallant manner and kissed her tiny hand, and told her to remember him, as well she may. I sat between the Duke of Buccleuch and Frederick Villiers at dinner, and had such a long talk with the Duke of Wellington afterwards ; he was so kind to me, and I have such an intense veneration for him, I always feel at least a foot taller whenever he notices me. He is looking very well, and rode part of the way with us yesterday, but he refrained from accompanying us all the time we drove, for the Queen drives so fast, it is very hard work riding by her carriage.

Windsor Castle, August 13, 1843.—The Queen walked for some time on the terrace this afternoon, and you never saw anything like the crowds of people. It was rather unpleasant when Her Majesty walked amongst them, for though the gentlemen tried to make way, the people pressed up so, it was difficult to keep them back. I suppose it is right that the Queen should show herself sometimes to her subjects, but I am always very glad when these walks are over. No one dined here last night except M. de Palmella, the Portuguese Minister. Next Thursday is the Duchess of Kent's birthday, and there is to be a large dinner at Frogmore, and a dance in the evening. I believe the Queen intends proroguing Parliament in person.

Windsor Castle, August 5, 1843.—Mr. Courtenay, the Queen's private chaplain, came yesterday, and we had family prayers for the first time. The chapel is not completed yet, so we met in the dining-room. I like Mr. Courtenay, and he reads remarkably well. I finished my letter yesterday in a desperate hurry, as we did not come home from driving till a quarter-past seven, and before dressing for dinner I had to make some wreaths of heather for our hair, which was gathered for us whilst we were out, by the Queen's desire. I just dressed in time; for whilst the last pin was being put in, I saw the Duchess of Kent's carriage driving up, so I rushed off, and was at the door to receive Her Royal Highness, though I had a good run for it. I enjoyed going over the state apartments yesterday, and seeing the beautiful pictures again, especially the Van Dykes, Claudes, and Rembrandts. I hope the whole of my waiting will be spent here; I revel in the beauty and repose of this lovely park, and I do not regret London at all. We drove for three hours yesterday. The afternoon was quite beautiful, and the lights and shades very strong. The trees are just beginning to lose the very cabbagy green of summer; and it is so pretty to see the deer among the ferns. Altogether, Windsor is certainly a princely possession, and I do not wonder at all foreigners being very much struck with its beauties. You will see by the papers that the party here received a considerable addition yesterday, as the Jerseys, Lord Somers, and Caroline Cocks came, and there was a dance in the evening. The two Lord Clintons, who are twin brothers, came to it, and are so alike, there is no knowing which is which. They are in the same regiment, and consequently wear the same uniform; and as they are the same height, complexion, &c., they are perfect fac-similes. Clemmy Villiers is looking very pretty. I hear Lord March's marriage to Miss Greville is just settled. I rode with the Queen yesterday, and Sydney Herbert took me in to dinner. I sat between him and the Duke of Buccleuch, which was very pleasant. Baron Gersdorff and his bride are here.

Windsor Castle, August 18, 1843.—I was so much amused at your saying in your letter yesterday that you were obliged to get up at six o'clock A.M. to get a good start from Newark; and this you call taking the journey easy! It seems to me that after great exertion, considerable fatigue, and travelling from morning till night, you had travelled about fifty miles. We dined at Frogmore last night, to celebrate the Duchess of Kent's birthday, and there was a dance in the evening. We ended it with a curious dance called

Grand-père, which is a sort of 'follow my leader.' The Prince and the Duchess of Kent led the way; and it was great fun, but rather a romp.

Windsor Castle, August 22, 1843.—We were kept waiting a long time yesterday for the French Princes, who arrived at last. The Prince de Joinville is tall, dark, and good-looking, with a large beard, and his hair rather in the 'Jeune France' style, but not exaggerated. He has a little look of Mario; but unfortunately he is terribly deaf, and it is with the greatest effort he can be made to hear anything. The Duc d'Aumale is much shorter, and very fair. We were rather amused yesterday at seeing them arrive in full uniform; though the gentlemen who went to meet them assured them it was not usual, they insisted upon stopping at the Embassy in London to dress.

Windsor Castle, August 23, 1843.—I never saw the Duke of Wellington looking better, and he was in such spirits.

Windsor Castle, August 24, 1843.—The Queen went to London yesterday, and we had such a pleasant little dinner at Frogmore. I sat next the Duchess of Kent, and she was so very kind and good-natured. After dinner she made us play some duets, and then she asked me to sing, which

I did. Then she sang a great deal herself—I accompanied Her Royal Highness; and the evening slipped away very pleasantly. The Duchess must have had a very fine voice, and now it is very true, and a pretty tone. She has kindly lent me her MS. book.

I have just been seeing two pictures of the Queen and Prince, by Winterhalter, in their robes, which promise to be very like. I find I do not like his former picture of the Queen as much as I did, for it is very cold and leaden in colour; but it is certainly very like, and I think Winterhalter catches the expression of the Queen's mouth better than anybody. It is peculiar, and very difficult to render without being a caricature.

Windsor Castle, August 26, 1843.—We drove with the Queen and the little Princess yesterday. The latter chattered the whole time, and was very amusing. Prince Albert rode away to look at a house he is having built, and the carriage stood still till he returned. The Queen was talking to us, and not taking any notice of the Princess, who suddenly exclaimed, 'There's a cat under the trees'—fertile imagination on her part, as there was nothing of the kind; but having succeeded in attracting attention, she quietly said, 'Cat come out to look at the Queen, I suppose.' Then she took a fancy to some heather at the side of the road, and asked Lady Dunmore to get her some. Lady Dunmore observed she could not do that, as we were driving too fast; so the Princess answered, 'No, *you* can't; but *those girls* might get out and get me some'—meaning Miss Paget and me!

Windsor Castle, August 27, 1843.—How little does one ever know what a day may bring forth! When I went to bed last night I thought as little about accompanying the Queen in her yachting expedition as you did; but Lady Canning came to my room early this morning to say that Lady Caroline Cocks had been sent for express, as her sister, who has long been delicate, was taken ill just after Lady Caroline left yesterday, and she feared she would not arrive in time to find her sister alive; so the Queen has asked me to take her waiting, and of course I must do so. I hope you will not worry yourself; the yacht is a beautiful boat, and I shall like seeing all the places, particularly as I believe (but this is as yet a grand secret) that the Queen is going to pay Louis Philippe a visit at the Château d'Eu.

We start to-morrow at seven, embark at Southampton, sail round the Isle of Wight; then go to Plymouth, Falmouth, and Eu ; and are to be back at Brighton by September 8. It is a great comfort that I shall be with dear Lady Canning ; she is so nice and kind, and such a good sailor, I am sure to be well taken care of.

CHAPTER IV.

Yachting with Her Majesty—The Isle of Wight, Dartmouth, Plymouth, and Falmouth—Visit to the Château d'Eu—Return to Windsor—General Colbert—Queen's Visit to Drayton, Chatsworth, and Belvoir—Music with the Queen—Visit to the Poultry Yard—Opening of the Chapel at Windsor—Visit of the Indian Chiefs.

Royal Yacht Victoria and Albert, Monday, August 28, 1843.—I left Windsor at half-past 7 A.M., in the same carriage as the Queen, Prince Albert, and Lady Canning, joined the railroad at Farnborough, and reached Southampton a quarter before 11 A.M. We embarked at once, and remained on deck in spite of the rain which fell in torrents. At three Her Majesty landed at Ryde, and we drove to St. Clare to pay Lady Katharine Harcourt a visit, returned on board at five, and anchored off Cowes for the night. Mr. Warren, one of the midshipmen, fell overboard at Ryde, but was not hurt; he dived under the vessel, and came up looking like a dripping spaniel. The sea was perfectly smooth. The party on board consisted of Her Majesty, Prince Albert, Lady

Canning, Lord Liverpool, Lord Aberdeen, Sir James Clarke, and myself; Lord Adolphus Fitzclarence in command of the ship.

Tuesday, 29th.—Passed a good night, my cabin small but comfortable. Her Majesty went in the barge at 8 A.M., rowed about Cowes Harbour, and went on board Lady Yarborough's yacht. We landed at East Cowes and drove to Norris Castle, which belonged to Mr. Bell, the editor of the weekly paper. The inmates were not dressed, but a lady received us, and Her Majesty walked on the terrace, saw some of the rooms, and appeared much interested in revisiting the scenes of her childhood. She spent three months at Norris as Princess Victoria in 1831, and again three months there in 1833; and when the place was for sale after Lord Henry Seymour's death, the Queen would have been glad to purchase it, but informed us she had not the means of doing so. At 10 A.M. we returned to the yacht, and weighed anchor soon after; the wind S.W., a strong breeze and heavy swell off the Needles; every one rather ill except Lady Canning. I remained in my cabin lying down till we anchored in Portland Roads. The Prince went on shore in the barge, the Queen did not leave the yacht.

Wednesday, 30th.—Weighed anchor before

8 A.M. The sea calm; there was a swell, but very little wind. About 11.30 I went on deck, found Her Majesty had passed a good night and was perfectly well; the Prince rather uncomfortable, but not ill. We lunched at one, and then went into Dartmouth Harbour, which is beautiful. The situation of the town is very striking; the houses are built up the cliffs, and the old church at the entrance of the harbour is most picturesque. Crowds of people came to the sides of the yacht in boats, and the quays were filled with the inhabitants waving flags and banners, and cheering enthusiastically. Her Majesty was rowed about the harbour in the barge, and the weather was very propitious. We weighed anchor at 3 P.M. and arrived at Plymouth at six, having gone thirteen knots an hour. I remained on deck most of the day, and sat for an hour with the Queen, who was well and in good spirits. The evening was beautiful, and the entrance into Plymouth very striking. There were several ships of war in the harbour which saluted, and many thousands of people lined the shore, which rises like an amphitheatre. Many boats came off, and Lord Haddington came on board.

Thursday, 31st.—Her Majesty went on shore in the barge at 8.30 A.M., and landed at Mount

Edgecumbe. There was a thick mist when first we landed, but it soon cleared off, and we drove in pony carriages to the church, then to the gardens, where we got out and walked. The evergreens are very fine, and grow most luxuriantly. The orange trees are the largest I ever saw in England. The Queen made a small collection of flowers at each place we went to, which were dried and kept as mementos. The arbutus drive is quite beautiful, and the views of the sea between the magnificent fir trees most striking. Lady Canning remarked that it reminded her of the Corniche; the pines give a peculiar richness to the landscape, which is unlike the general character of England. We returned on board shortly before eleven. The Prince visited the docks, and at three we accompanied the Queen to Plymouth. The Lords of the Admiralty received Her Majesty, who drove round the town in an open landau, attended by the Prince, Lady Canning, and myself. The crowds were immense, and we had no cavalry escort, but soldiers marched on each side of the carriage, and the officers escorted us. Sometimes the pressure was so great, the infantry bayonets crossed in the carriage, which was rather unpleasant; but the people on the whole behaved very well, and cheered most enthusiastically. Such a tremendous crush is, however, always disagreeable, and it was a great relief when the drive was over. The sun was very powerful, and the heat intense. The Queen went on board the 'Caledonian,' a magnificent ship of war, 110 guns. She was just ready to sail. The Admiral, Sir David Milne, received us, and Lord and Lady Morley were on board. We dined with the Queen, and afterwards remained on deck a considerable time.

Friday, September 1.—We weighed anchor at 8.30, and steamed out of the harbour, five men-of-war saluting, and their yards manned, a very pretty sight. The day was beautiful and the sea like glass, which enabled us to pass within pistol-shot of the Eddystone Lighthouse, and we arrived at Falmouth at 2 P.M. The Queen was rowed round the harbour in the barge, and the crowd of people was awful. Vessels and boats of every description, large and small, filled to the utmost, and the moment they caught sight of the royal barge the people seemed to lose their heads completely, left the helms to take care of themselves, and rushed to the side of the vessel nearest the barge, so that it was really alarming, and the Queen expressed great anxiety for her loyal subjects. The eight men-of-war boats which accompanied us were quite cut off from us, and at one moment the barge was completely jammed. Fortunately, as soon as he saw an opening, Lord Adolphus ordered the men to pull away as hard as they could, and we out-distanced the pleasure boats and got safe back to the yacht; where the Queen received the Mayor, who being a Quaker, asked permission to remain with his hat on. We left Falmouth at a quarter past three, and sailed for Cherbourg. I remained on deck a long time with Her Majesty, and she taught me to plait paper for bonnets, which was a favourite occupation of the Queen's. Lady Canning and I had settled ourselves in a very sheltered place, protected by the paddle-box, and when we had been there some time the Queen came on deck, and remarking what a comfortable spot we had chosen, Her Majesty sent for her camp stool and settled herself beside us, plaiting away most composedly, when suddenly we observed a commotion among the sailors, little knots of men talking together in a mysterious manner: first one officer came up to them, then another, they looked puzzled, and at last Lord Adolphus Fitzclarence was called. The Queen, much *intriguée*, asked what was the matter, and inquired whether we were going to have a mutiny on board. Lord Adolphus laughed, but remarked he really did not know what *would* happen unless Her Majesty would be graciously pleased to move her seat. 'Move my seat,' said the Queen, 'why should I? what possible harm can I be doing here?' 'Well, ma'am,' said Lord Adolphus, 'the fact is, your Majesty is unwittingly closing up the door of the place where the grog tubs are kept, and so the men cannot have their grog!' 'Oh, very well,' said the Queen, 'I will move on one condition, viz., that you bring me a glass of grog.' This was accordingly done, and after tasting it the Queen said, 'I am afraid I can only make the same remark I did once before, that I think it would be very good if it were stronger!' This of course delighted the men, and the little incident caused much amusement on board.

The sunset was clear and very beautiful, and the Queen desired that the sailors should dance on deck. Lady Canning and I went on deck after dinner; the sea was perfectly smooth, and we saw several porpoises which followed the ship at a distance.

Saturday, September 2.—I was called before six, and as soon as I was dressed I went on deck, where I found the Queen and the Prince de Joinville, who had come on board attended by two gentlemen.

The day was beautiful. We passed Cherbourg at some little distance, but could distinguish the breakwater and forts with a telescope. The Prince de Joinville told us of a narrow escape the French royal family had on Monday last. They were visiting a small fortress; the King, the Queen, and all the royal family, except the Duc de Nemours, were in a large carriage. They were passing a drawbridge when a salute was fired, which frightened the horses, one of which jumped over the side, dragging two others with it. Luckily the carriage caught against the rail, and the traces gave way, otherwise in all probability the whole party would have been killed.

We lunched at one; and then the Queen sent for us, and we remained on deck the rest of the afternoon. Soon after three we passed Dieppe, which we saw clearly; and then shortly we came in sight of Eu, which we reached at 5.30. As soon as the royal yacht approached, the King, Louis Philippe, accompanied by the Duc d'Aumale and the Duc de Montpensier, Lord Cowley, and several of the suite put off in the royal barge, and immediately came on board the yacht. The King embraced the Queen on both cheeks, and then kissed Her Majesty's hand, and welcomed her most heartily to the shores of

CHATEAU D'EU

France. The first time an English sovereign had visited France since the Field of the Cloth of Gold. At first the King seemed quite overcome; but he soon recovered himself, and spoke to us all in excellent English. He is very like the impression on the French coins—stout, with a good countenance; his hair, which is thick and grizzly, brushed up in a point, and his complexion florid. The Queen went on shore with His Majesty in his barge, and we followed immediately in the Queen's; and when we landed we found the Queen and Prince, and the whole French royal family, under a large canopy close to the shore. There were present Louis Philippe and Queen Marie Amélie, the Queen of the Belgians, Madame Adélaide, the King's old sister, the Prince and Princess de Joinville, the poor Duchess of Orléans, Prince and Princess Augustus of Saxe-Coburg, the Dukes d'Aumale and Montpensier, Lord and Lady Cowley and their daughter Miss Wellesley, Madame Vilain XIV., Madame Angelet, Mademoiselle de Chabot, and the rest of the suite. The Queen of the French and all the royalties received us most graciously. Queen Marie Amélie has a charming countenance, which, however, bears the impression of deep grief, and it is said she will never recover the death of the Duc d'Orléans, who was her favourite son. The Duchess is still in deep mourning, and it was very sad to see her. The entrance to the town of Eu, which is a small watering-place, is most picturesque; the old church rises above the town on a high hill, and on this occasion the quantity of troops, the masses of people all dressed in their holiday clothes, and the women in their white caps, added very much to the brilliancy of the scene. The procession was curious, and quite mediæval. The Queen, Prince Albert, and all the French royal family entered a large *char-à-bancs*, with a canopy and curtains, which were left open. This vehicle was drawn by twelve large clumsy horses, caparisoned; there was a coachman on the box, and three footmen behind in state liveries, besides a motley crew of outriders, of every size and description, mounted on wretched horses, and dressed in many different liveries. This *char-à-bancs* was followed by eight others, drawn by eight horses, and accompanied by a large escort of cavalry; and all the road was lined with troops. The Château d'Eu rather resembles the architecture of the Tuileries, and is interesting from having been the scene of many historical events. William the Conqueror was married at Eu, and it was long the residence of the Ducs de Guise. No doubt the Queen's visit will add to its interest to succeeding generations.

The long procession winding through the avenue looked most picturesque, and reminded me of the pictures of the time of Louis XIV. The square in front of the Palace was lined with troops, and on our arrival the King and Queen Victoria showed themselves on the balcony. We then attended Her Majesty to her rooms, which were elegantly furnished with beautiful Beauvais tapestry, parquet floors, painted ceilings, and the pictures which were saved by the fidelity of servants during the French Revolution, and afterwards restored to their rightful owners. Our rooms were at the top of the house, immediately over the Queen's—comfortable and convenient in every respect; Lady Canning's and mine close together.

We dressed in a great hurry for dinner, and went down to the Queen's sitting-room, where presently the Royal family assembled. There was a very large dinner-party; and I sat next Marshal Sebastiani and le Ministre des Marines. I was amused by seeing my opposite neighbour, with whom I had not made acquaintance, nodding at me; and presently a message came to ask me to drink wine with General d'Houdetot, which it seems he thought was an English custom.

After dinner we waited for a short time in an ante-drawing-room; but were soon sent for to sit at the Royal table, where I was placed next the King, who was exceedingly civil; but I was so intensely sleepy, from having been up unusually early and spending the whole day on deck, that it was positive pain to me to keep my eyes open and hide my yawns. The young Princesse de Joinville, who had lately arrived from the Brazils, was very pretty; but evidently disliked the formality of Court life, and at times could scarcely refrain from showing how bored she was by it. She told me she had never seen snow, and could not imagine what it is like.

We retired about eleven, and I was most thankful to go to bed, after a day of considerable fatigue and excitement.

Sunday, September 3.—I was up before seven, and, as there was no Protestant Church, Lady Canning and I read the Church Service together; after which we went down to what was called breakfast, where the whole party assembled. We were served with soup, fish, made dishes, puddings, fruit, and then tea and coffee. We afterwards spent some time in the drawing-room, and at half-past three we all went out driving in the *chars-à-bancs*, not, however, before we saw the private apartments of the Royal family and the Chapel, which is beautiful. We were shown some very fine point lace, which had belonged to Cardinal Richelieu, and a vestment which had been embroidered by Mademoiselle de Montpensier. The walls were covered with historical portraits; but few appeared to be originals. We drove through the farm and over some high ground, and returned by Tréport. The roads were atrocious—so narrow there was scarcely room for the *chars-à-bancs*, immensely deep ruts, and huge stones—in short, they were more like the beds of mountain torrents than roads in a civilised country. We were bumped and shaken to pieces; and even in the pleasure-grounds of the Château the roads are so narrow, and the turns so excessively sharp, that I was quite glad when the Queen got safe back.

At dinner I sat between Lord Aberdeen and Lord Charles Wellesley. I was informed there was to have been a theatrical performance that evening, but the Queen of the Belgians told the King that in England it is not customary to have either a play or a concert on Sunday. The Royal family attended Mass daily at 10 o'clock A.M., before breakfast; and I was rather surprised to see that the King and Queen both carved at dinner.

Monday, the 4th, I came up to my room immediately after breakfast, as, besides my own letters, the Queen gave me some writing to do, which occupied me till half-past one, when we all went out again in six *chars-à-bancs*, and drove over more bad roads to the Forest. Part of the drive was pretty; but the carriage was so rough I was glad when, at the end of nearly three hours, we stopped to lunch in a large tent which had been put up in an open spot in the Forest, surrounded by the King's Guards and a crowd of the inhabitants of Tréport and its neighbourhood assembled.

A band played during luncheon, after which the King and Queen Victoria walked about arm-in-arm. We then returned home, and reached the Château about six o'clock. There was, as usual, a large dinner-party of above seventy people, and after dinner a beautiful instrumental concert, conducted by Auber. The King had sent for the Corps de l'Opéra, in order to have an opera; but, unfortunately, they only brought two pieces—one ridiculed the English, and the other was said to be so improper that the Queen objected to it; so we had to content ourselves with the musical performance, which was very good, and well executed. We did not retire till past midnight.

Tuesday, September 5.—Prince Albert reviewed the troops; but returned to breakfast. We sat in the drawing-room till 12.30, when I went out sketching with Lady Canning. At half-past three we went to see the old church, which is exceedingly fine. In passing the Chapel of the Virgin, Queen Amélie and her daughter knelt down and prayed for some minutes. In one of the chapels there is a curious group in marble, representing the entombment of our Lord, surrounded by the Marys and two of the disciples.

We afterwards descended to the crypt, where there are the ancient monuments of the Comtes d'Eu; they had recently been repaired, and are curious. The place was lighted with candles, and was exceedingly picturesque. The poor Duchesse d'Orléans went down with us, but was so overcome she was obliged to leave us; and when we returned into the body of the church, we found her and the Queen of the Belgians prostrate before one of the altars, and the Duchess was weeping bitterly. She had never appeared in public since the Duke's death till the Queen's arrival, and when she was seen for the first time and was received with acclamations of 'Vive la Duchesse d'Orléans!' she was completely overcome. She seemed a most amiable, charming person, and her two little boys were very pretty children. After seeing the church, we drove in *chars-à-bancs* to Tréport, where an immense multitude had collected, as it was rumoured that the Queen intended going on board the yacht. The sea was, however, too rough; so we returned to Eu, and walked round the gardens and home through the pleasure-grounds. I was shown two beech trees, which existed in the time of the Guises, and it is said the League was signed under their boughs. There was the usual large dinner party, and another fine instrumental concert in the evening.

Wednesday, September 6.—After breakfast, Lady Canning and I went out sketching till two, when the whole party drove again sixteen miles into the forest, to the house of one of the *Gardes-à-Chasse.* The mansion was in a dilapidated condition, but commanded a fine view; and we found an excellent luncheon spread out under some fine old beech trees. A good many people assembled, and the afternoon was very bright and beautiful. As the distance was so great, post-horses met us half-way; and the Queen was very much struck and amused at the curious costume of the postillions, who wore glazed hats trimmed with tricolour ribbons, yellow breeches, and huge boots; the harness was rope, and very primitive. We did not get back to Eu till 6.30, when we immediately dressed for dinner; and in the evening there was a pretty French play, called 'Le Château de ma Nièce,' and a vaudeville after it. The actors and actresses all came from Paris.

Thursday, September 7.—I was called at 5 A.M., and saw the sun rise. The morning was lovely. We all breakfasted together at 6.30; and left the Château, as we had arrived, in seven *chars-à-bancs* with an escort. The Queen, Prince Albert, and all the French Royal family went in the King's barge, and we followed in Her Majesty's. The entrance out of the harbour was exceedingly narrow, and I was completely deafened by the noise of the salutes as we passed; but was struck by the different tones of the guns, some were so much shriller and sharper than others. The King remained rather more than a quarter of an hour on board, and then took an affectionate leave.

Our vessel weighed anchor; and we reached Brighton after a prosperous voyage, accompanied by the Prince de Joinville, who was much excited by a race between his ship and the 'Black Eagle,' in which the English boat had decidedly the best of it, and out-distanced the French boat, to the Prince's extreme disgust. He remarked upon the respectful silence which was observed on board the Queen's yacht, and said how impossible it would be to prevent French sailors from talking.

The Queen of the French gave me a pretty jacinth and diamond bracelet; and nothing could have been kinder than all the ladies-in-waiting, especially Mademoiselle de Chabot, Madame de Rouille, Madame de Rumigny, and Madame Vilain XIV., whom I shall ever remember with feelings of gratitude and pleasure.

Windsor Castle, November 25, 1843.—'The Duc de Nemours is at Melton, the Duchess is here, and as pretty and nice as ever; but poor thing, she has had a bad account of her little son the Comte d'Eu, which makes her very anxious; I trust his indisposition is only caused by teething, for when I saw him he looked the nicest, healthiest, little fellow possible! Lord Lincoln was the only stranger at dinner yesterday; he made such kind inquiries after you and papa, and said he could never forget your kindness to him and his children, and he should so like you to see them again.

Windsor Castle, November 25.—I sat last night at dinner next old General Colbert, who was one of Napoleon's Generals, and also his Chambellan. He is such a nice old man, and likes talking of his campaigns, so I made him tell me about the retreat from Russia, burning of Moscow, &c., and he was most agreeable. He being then a commanding officer did not suffer as much as many from the hardships of that terrible retreat; but he marched for one hundred and five days, fifteen hours a day, always expecting to be pursued, when it would have been a case of *sauve qui peut*. I told him of the curious drawing we have at Ravensworth of the Emperor Napoleon by Isabey, and he said he had no doubt it was very like, for that Isabey lived so much with the Emperor, he had many opportunities of studying his countenance; but he did not believe the Emperor actually sat for his picture more than once, and that was to David.

Beckett, December 6, 1843.—I hear from Minnie (Marchioness of Normanby) that everything went off beautifully at Chatsworth during the Queen's visit, and the illuminations and fireworks were lovely. The Queen was very much pleased, and the Duke of Devonshire was in the highest spirits at the way everything answered. I have had a long amusing account from Matilda Paget of the visit to Drayton, which seems to have gone off so well that the Peels have every reason to be satisfied.

It is fortunate that the weather has been so much

finer than could have been expected at this season of the year. I must leave this early to-morrow to be at Windsor to receive my Royal Mistress, as she always starts early. Do not call Windsor 'my triste Palace,' as I am always very happy there. The Queen's good fortune with regard to weather is quite remarkable. She yachts during the equinox, and has the sea as calm as a mirror the whole time; she visits about in the dead of winter, and has the brightest sunshine and weather we should often rejoice to have in summer!

George Barrington came over here to hunt yesterday, and brought eight Oxford friends with him to dinner. I knew Lord Lascelles and Lord Clifden, and made Lord Belgrave's acquaintance, but he was very shy, and this is his first term at college.

Extracts of Letters from the Hon. Matilda Paget during the Queen's Visit to Drayton, Chatsworth, and Belvoir.

Drayton, November 29, 1843.—I must tell you how well everything has gone off hitherto. Before dinner Lady Peel and all the ladies waited for the Queen, and then Lady Peel presented a lovely bouquet. Several addresses were read.

I went in to dinner with the Duke of Wellington, the Duke of Buccleuch sat on my other side, but I luckily had the Duke of Wellington's *good* ear, so I did very well. He had been at Lord March's wedding (the present Duke of Richmond, who married Miss Greville), had a favour in his button hole, told me all about it, and was very good-natured. I like Lady Peel—she is so truly kind. The Queen has looked pleased and happy, and it has not been the least formal. The Queen played at patience with the ladies, the gentlemen stood about. The Queen looked very nice in a pink silk gown with three flounces. We sat in a charming library—a most perfect and pretty room, with two fire-places, opening into a hall with a billiard table, where there were beautiful statues and pictures. I think Sir Robert and Lady Peel must be quite satisfied: the dinner was very well done, and Sir Robert proposed the healths.

Drayton, Wednesday, November 29.—We breakfasted at ten, and at half-past the Queen and all the ladies went out walking, and visited the farm, dairy, kitchen garden, &c., all very nice and in good order, but nothing *fine*. When we came in the Queen went over the house, and was especially diverted at my room, because the

Imperial nearly prevented her coming in. The Prince is gone to Birmingham, and has got a fine bright day. The Queen Dowager is to arrive to-day, and to-morrow the Queen is going to see Lichfield Cathedral. After luncheon to-day we sauntered about in the hall, and looked over some books of engravings.

The Duchess of Buccleuch wore such a lovely gown made of some old brocaded silk that belonged to the Duke's great, great aunt—it was very beautiful.

Chatsworth, December 1, 1843.—The grandeur of this place far surpasses anything I could have imagined. When we arrived at Chesterfield, the Duke of Devonshire received the Queen, who immediately started in a coach and six. We followed in a coach and four. I have just returned from seeing Haddon Hall, with Lady Mary Howard, Ladies Palmerston and Melbourne, and General Wemyss. It was very beautiful and interesting, but I cannot attempt to enter into details till we meet. The party here consists of the Duke of Wellington, Duke and Duchess of Buccleuch, Lord and Lady Emlyn, Colonel Cavendish and his son, Mr. Charles and Lady Katherine Cavendish and their son and daughter, Mr. and Mrs. Brand, Duke and Duchess of Bedford, Lords Palmerston, Melbourne and Alvanley, Lord and Lady Normanby, Lord and Lady Leveson, and Mr. Frederic Leveson, Charles Gore, Mr. and Lady Louisa Cavendish, Mr. and Lady Emily Cavendish, and Alfred Paget. Lady Normanby is more dear and kind than I can describe. This morning she asked me to walk with her, and we went off to the conservatory, which is too lovely. At half-past one the Queen and Prince went over the State rooms with the Duke, then after luncheon we drove out, and at half-past six we all went to see the conservatory lighted up—some in carriages, some walking. The ball last night was very pretty, in a grand banquetting hall with a rococo ceiling. Mrs. Arkwright was there, and was taken up and presented to the Queen, who talked to her for some time. This evening there have been lovely fireworks, the cascades and fountains all lighted up with red and green lights, which had a fairy-like effect. I was so amused at the Duke of Devonshire coming up to me in the middle of it all, when everyone was so amazed and excited and saying, in an insinuating voice, 'Do you like my *little* fireworks?' I went into dinner with Lord Beauvale, and his wife is charming. The Queen is well, and danced the country dance with Lord

Leveson with much vigour, and Her Majesty waltzed with the Prince. The royal magnificence of everything here is overpowering. No other place can come up to it. On Sunday there were prayers at eleven, and then we went to the kitchen garden. In the evening we walked through the statue gallery and conservatory, and there was some delightful music performed by the Duke's own band—some of Rossini's 'Stabat Mater,' the 'Creation,' &c. Lady Normanby protected me, and (as you were not there) called me her child. She is so clever and well informed, and yet there is that about her which prevents one feeling ashamed of one's ignorance. The Queen left Chatsworth at nine, and the Duke of Devonshire, who accompanied Her Majesty as far as Derby, was in the highest spirits, and delighted at the way everything had gone off. At Chesterfield I helped the Queen to get *up on a chair*, that Her Majesty might look out of a very high window. She took such very tight hold of my hand to prevent herself falling, that one saw Her Majesty is evidently not used to getting on chairs! The crowds at Derby and Nottingham were perfectly astonishing, especially at the latter place, which was more like Edinburgh than anything else, and we arrived here (Belvoir Castle, December 4) at half-past one. The party here is the Queen Dowager, Duke of Wellington, Duke and Duchess of Bedford, Lord and Lady Hardwicke, Sir Robert and Lady Peel, Mr. and Lady Emmeline Wortley, Lord and Lady Katherine Jermyn, Mr. and Lady Elizabeth Drummond, Lord Granby and Forester, &c., and dear old Lord Charles Manners, who was my father's best friend. To-morrow the Prince is to go out hunting, and the hounds meet here.

Windsor Castle, December 9, 1843.—No one dined here last night except the Duchess of Kent, and her lady in waiting, Lady Fanny Howard, so we all sat at the Queen's table after dinner, who was very chatty and in good spirits. She told me she had met two of my sisters during her tour, Lady Normanby at Chatsworth and Lady Hardwicke at Belvoir. The Prince talked a great deal, and both he and the Queen told some funny anecdotes. One was that the mother of a girl who was going into service in a Duke's establishment gave her daughter strict injunctions to say 'Your Grace,' if ever the Duke spoke to her. The girl promised to pay attention to this, and departed. A few days afterwards the Duke met her in a passage and asked her some question, which instead of answering, the poor girl immediately began, 'For what I have received,' etc.

On another occasion, an Inspector was examining the children at the Duke's school. Among other questions he asked the meaning of the word 'grace,' upon which the children all exclaimed with one accord that it meant the Duke of Rutland!

Windsor Castle, December 12, 1843.—We had such a delightful practice for nearly two hours yesterday afternoon with the Queen and Prince Albert on two pianofortes. We played a fine, but a very difficult duet of Beethoven's. The time was so difficult one requires to be a good musician to understand it. To-night I am to sing with the Queen, and I have got a great heap of music to practise the seconds. I always like playing and singing with Her Majesty, and am very glad the Queen has begun doing so again. The private band last night played a magnificent composition of Spohr's, the 'Creation of Sound,' very learned, but very fine. It is divided into four movements. The first is intended to represent the first awakening of life after the creation of sound—and the voices of nature are very grand indeed—; but the third movement of martial music and a march to battle is one of the finest things I ever heard in my life. It is so difficult that the band of the Philharmonic, supposed to be one of the best in Europe, could not learn it till Spohr came over himself to explain it. The Prince showed me the score, there are four different times going on at once, and I got as puzzled as I do when you tell me about the second marriage of my grandfather's fifth cousin with my great uncle's sister-in-law, which makes me first cousin once removed to his children.

Windsor Castle, December 15, 1843.—I went to the Queen's room yesterday, and saw her before we began to sing. She was so thoroughly kind and gracious. The music went off very well, Costa accompanied, and I was pleased by the Queen's telling me, when I asked whether I had not better practise the things a little more, that 'that was not necessary, as I knew them perfectly.' She also said, 'If it was *convenient* to me I was to go down to her room any evening to try the Masses.' Just as if anything she desired could be *inconvenient.* However, I said of course I should be only too happy, but at the same time I hinted at the possibility of my coming down at a wrong moment, so then Her Majesty said she should send for me, and if I was at home I might go to her. It did make me laugh in my sleeve, because except when I went to St. George's by no chance do I ever go anywhere. I was reminded of the scene in Hamlet—

> *Queen.* If it will please you
> To show us so much gentry and good will
> As to expend your time with us awhile,
> For the supply and profit of our hope,
> Your visitation shall receive such thanks
> As fits a king's remembrance.
> *Rosen.* Both your majesties
> Might, by the sovereign power you have of us,
> Put your dread pleasures more into command
> Than to entreaty.
> *Guil.* But we both obey,
> And here give up ourselves, in the full bent
> To lay our service freely at your feet,
> To be commanded.—*Hamlet*, Act II. Sc. 2.

We had a pleasant interview with the Royal children in Lady Lyttelton's room yesterday, and *almost* a romp with the Princess Royal and the Prince of Wales. They had got a round ivory counter which I spun for them, and they went into such fits of laughter it did my heart good to hear them. The Princess Royal is wonderfully quick and clever. She is always in the Queen's room when we play or sing, and she seems especially fond of music, and stands listening most attentively without moving. Last night one of the pianofortes had been taken out of the room. The Queen left the Princess with me for a short time, so she said, 'Where's the other pianoforte gone, they have taken it away?' So I answered, 'Yes, ma'am, for we are going to sing to-night, not play.' 'Oh, *you* are going to sing, and where is Miss Paget, not coming? Oh, only you sing with papa and mamma.'

Lady Lyttelton told us that a certain Major Douglas had sent the Princess some beautiful toys a long time ago, so the other day he had an audience, and before he left the Queen desired the little Princess to thank him for them, which she accordingly did very nicely, and when Lady Lyttelton took her down again to the Queen's room, she mentioned in an undertone that the child had delivered her speech very well, so the Queen turned round to her and said, 'Well, pussy, and what did you say?' The Princess answered, 'I said—I said my speech.'

Windsor Castle, December 18, 1843.—We walked with the Queen and Prince yesterday to the Home farm, saw the turkeys crammed, looked at the pigs, and then went to see the new aviary, where there is a beautiful collection of pigeons, fowls, etc. etc., of rare kinds. The pigeons are so tame they will perch upon Prince Albert's hat, and the Queen's shoulders. It was funny seeing the Royal pair amusing themselves with farming! When we came home, we examined the busts and pictures in the corridor, and I heard more about them than I ever did before. The Queen gave me such a good autograph yesterday, and I have got several interesting additions to my collection. The private chapel is to be consecrated to-morrow at twelve o'clock by the Bishop of Oxford, who came here yesterday; and Lady Douro is coming for her first waiting. I was sitting in Matilda Paget's room yesterday, and we were just going to dress for dinner, when in rushed Miss——. She had come down to Windsor with two friends of hers—a newly married couple—and she had been all over the Castle and St. George's Chapel; and in less than five minutes she recounted the whole history—chronological, historical, and genealogical—of her friend and his wife, and all their ancestors on both sides, that she had brought them to Windsor, and done this and that, and everything, and that they were having tea in Lady Portman's room, and she wanted us to go and look at them. She sent us into such fits of laughing; and as for Lord Morton, who had never seen her before, he could scarcely believe his senses. I never knew such an original as she is, exactly like Miss Pratt in the 'Inheritance.' Lord Melbourne and the Beauvales go away to-day. The former was not well yesterday, and had a slight touch of gout; it always makes me sad to see him, he is so changed.

Windsor Castle, December 19, 1843.—My waiting is nearly over, and though I shall be delighted to get home, I always regret leaving my dear kind mistress, particularly when I have been a good deal with Her Majesty, as I have been this waiting. We sang again last night, and after Costa went away, I sorted a quantity of music for the Queen; and then Prince Albert said he had composed a German ballad, which he thought would suit my voice, and he wished me to sing it. So His Royal Highness accompanied me, and I sang it at sight, which rather alarmed me, but I got through it, and it is very pretty. The Duchess of Kent has promised to have it copied for me. The Prince of Wales stayed some time in the room whilst we were practising. He was very attentive, and both he and the Princess Royal seem to have a decided taste for music. We sang some of my beloved Masses (Mozart's), and you cannot think how beautiful they are with all the parts filled up. Costa had composed a very pretty Miserere, which we also sang.

Windsor Castle, December 20, 1843.—The Chapel was consecrated yesterday. The service was performed partly by the Bishop of Oxford and partly by Mr. Courtenay. I thought it a beautiful and impressive service, and the Bishop read so remarkably well. Lady Douro arrived, and has brought her harp, so we played some duets yesterday evening, and were in the middle of one when the Queen sent for me to play with her. I was pleased at going the last evening, because it seemed as if Her Majesty was satisfied and wished to continue playing with me as long as possible. We dine at Frogmore, and in the afternoon the Indian Chiefs come to see the Queen. When we were playing with the Queen yesterday, the news arrived of poor old Lord Lynedoch's death at the age of ninety-two. The Queen and Prince were quite grieved about it. I had not a very good account of Lord Grey yesterday from Lady Georgiana. He continues extremely unwell, though they hope he may recover, if his strength can resist such protracted suffering, which I fear at his age is not likely.

Eight Indians of the Chippewa tribe came to see the Queen. They consisted of five chiefs, two women, a little girl, and a half-breed. Her Majesty received them in the Waterloo Gallery, and in consequence of the oldest chief, a fine old man of seventy-five, having a sore throat, the second chief made a speech, which was interpreted by Mr. Catlin. He began by saying 'He was much pleased that the Great Spirit had permitted them to cross the large lake (the Atlantic) in safety, that they had wished to see their great mother (the Queen). This they repeated three times with little variation. He then said that England was the great light of the world, and that its rays illuminated all nations, and reached even to their country. That they found it much larger than they expected, that the buildings were finer than theirs, and the wigwam (Windsor Castle) was very grand, and they were pleased to see it; that, nevertheless, they should return to their own country and be quite happy and contented; that they thanked the Great Spirit they had enough to eat—they were satisfied. They thought the people in England must be very rich, and they looked pleased and happy. They (the Chippewas) had served under our sovereigns, had fought their battles, and that he (the chief) had served under De Kinnsey, the greatest chief that had ever existed, or had ever been known. (Mr. Catlin observed, he supposed he had never heard of the Duke of Wellington, therefore he thought his general the greatest man.) He had been on the field of battle when his general was killed, and had helped to bury him. He had received kindness from our nation, for which he thanked us; their wigwams at home had been made comfortable with our things. He had nothing more to say. He had finished.'

When first they came in, Prince Albert shook hands with them all; they looked exceedingly grave, and were dressed with large bunches of feathers on their heads, their faces dreadfully tattooed, and they all had on large skins. The women have long black hair, and a dress which comes down to their feet. They had quantities of coloured beads hung about them, and one of them had a small looking-glass. They danced two war dances, one of the chiefs playing a sort of drum, which consisted of a tub with a piece of buffalo hide stretched over it. The shrieks and the noises they made were quite unnatural and terrific. They did not begin to dance at once, but seemed to wait till inspired, and began by shaking all their joints, then moving slowly, until at last they performed the most distorted and violent antics. The old chief remained seated on one side of the room, the women on the other. They had large clubs, tomahawks, wooden swords, bows and a spear, and during one of the dances one of them shook a sort of rattle. The Queen was much astonished and interested.

CHAPTER V.

Mesmerism—The Queen's Visit to the City ; opening of the Royal Exchange—Sir Robert Peel and Lord Ellenborough—Sir Robert and Lady Sale — The Queen's Rings — Review at Windsor—Queen's Visit to Burghley.

In the winter of 1844 my sister-in-law, Mrs. Thomas Liddell, having been much interested in the question of mesmerism, which was being practised by Miss Martineau at Tynemouth, in our neighbourhood, determined to try its effect upon a young maid of my mother's, who was suffering very much from palpitations. The soothing result upon her nervous system was very remarkable, and she showed evident signs of *clairvoyance.* The clergyman of our parish, the Rev. John Collinson, expressed doubts as to the truth of the fact, and asked permission to try the girl's powers. Mrs. Thomas Liddell said she had not the slightest objection to his doing so. Accordingly, in a few days he brought a sealed packet, no one in the house knowing what it contained, which he gave me ; and the first time the girl was mesmerised, my sister-in-law gave it into her hands, and said she wished to know what it was. The girl opened the packet, which contained a lock of hair; this she stroked for a few seconds, and then threw away, saying it was disagreeable to her, and there was no light in it. My sister-in-law picked it up and gave it back, saying, 'Oh, nonsense! I wish to know more about it.' The girl took the hair, shuddered, and again said, 'There's no light in it; it is the hair of a dead person, and of one who had a very terrible struggle before death.' The hair was again sealed up, and I gave the packet back to Mr. Collinson, who was much surprised, as he said it was all perfectly true. The hair had belonged to his daughter, who had died of galloping consumption about eighteen months previously, and who had had a most painful struggle before her death.

On another occasion, I had just returned from one of my waitings, and had brought with me a small prayer-book, which contained, at the end, the music of chants and hymns. It had only just been unpacked, so I am sure the girl had not seen it; and I took it up, quite accidentally, when I was going to the room where she was mesmerised. Her eyes were bandaged, and the book was put into her hands topsy-turvy. She felt the first page with the tips of her fingers, and then exclaimed, 'What a funny book! it has got music instead of words.' She always seemed to read with the tips of her fingers or the back of her head, and whenever, her eyes being bandaged, she was asked to tell the hour, she turned the back of her head towards the clock.

I have a horror of mesmerism, and have never seen it practised since that time; but can testify to the truth of these facts, and also to the extraordinary soothing power it had over the girl, who used to have such palpitations of the heart one could see the pulsations in her throat; but within three minutes of her being sent into the magnetic sleep, these palpitations ceased, and her pulse beat quietly and regularly. The doctor declared no power of medicine could have produced such a result as rapidly.

Windsor Castle, October 27, 1844.—I shall have but little time to write to-morrow, as we are to leave Windsor before 11 A.M. The Queen is to be at Temple Bar at twelve, and as the procession will go at a foot's-pace we shall be a long time driving there from Buckingham Palace.

A funny thing happened yesterday. Charles Murray being still confined to his room at Brighton, the equerry-in-waiting has to receive Her Majesty's orders every day about dinner, etc. etc. The Queen seldom dines in private two days running; so we were rather surprised when we were informed there was to be a household dinner in the oak room. Accordingly, punctually at eight, we sat down to dinner, and had just finished our soup and fish when a message came from the Queen to know who gave the order that we were to dine without her. We stared at each other, and at last it was discovered to be a mistake of one of the pages! We, however, finished our dinner, and adjourned to the drawing-room. Then we were told that Her Majesty was coming, the gentlemen being in plain evening coats. It suddenly struck us that it was very cool, to say the least of it, that we should be amusing ourselves in the drawing-room instead of waiting for the Queen in the corridor; so, accordingly, we all rushed off, and were only just in time to receive Her Majesty and the Prince, who seemed much entertained at the mistake, which made quite a little diversion in the regularity of the life at Court. It always strikes me as so odd when I come back into waiting: everything else changes, but the life here never does, and is always exactly the same from day to day and year to year. The

Queen and Prince stayed a long time in the corridor after church, and talked about the Tahiti affair, the coronation, and one or two more interesting subjects; and we were sent for yesterday to stay with Her Majesty whilst she was sitting to Thorburn. We saw Prince Alfred, who is a very fine child, and looks very healthy, plump, and rosy. He has large blue eyes, looks good natured—a real darling baby, and much the finest the Queen has had. Her Majesty had his cap taken off to show us his hair, which is very dark, but is growing lighter. When I tied it on again, the Queen laughed, and said to Lady Portman, 'Oh, Georgy understands all about babies, she has so many nephews and nieces; pray, how many have you now, my dear?' I answered I believed I had forty six, but I was not quite sure!

Windsor Castle, October 29, 1844.—Nothing could have gone off better than the event yesterday; and it was one of the most curious sights I ever witnessed. I am so glad I happened to be in waiting. To begin with, the procession to the city was magnificent—very much the same as that at the Coronation. I went in a state carriage with Lady Gardiner (the bedchamber woman-in-waiting), the Duke of Norfolk (Earl Marshal), and Lord Anglesea (Gold-stick). The procession began to move at eleven, and the weather, which in the early morning was rather thick and foggy, began to clear from that moment, and by the time we reached the Strand there was a blue sky and bright sunshine. I can give you no notion of the crowd ; even at the Coronation I never saw anything like it. From Buckingham Palace to the Royal Exchange every place, hole, or cranny which commanded the smallest view of the road was crammed to suffocation to such an extent that even the rafters erected over the temporary seats were covered with people, and I only wonder many were not crushed to death. At the same time, the perfect order that was preserved throughout was very remarkable and pleasing. I believe a good many special constables were sworn in for the occasion, and they were dressed in the great-coats of the police ; so it was lucky for the latter that the weather was so fine, otherwise the police would have come off second best. The Lord Mayor and Aldermen met the Queen at Temple Bar at twelve. We all arrived at the Royal Exchange before Her Majesty, who was in the famous glass coach, with the Prince and Lord Jersey, Master of the Horse, and Lady Canning (who, in the absence of the

Duchess of Buccleuch, acted as Mistress of the Robes). As soon as Her Majesty alighted, she walked round the Colonnade, and then through the inner court, which is of course in the open air; so we had reason to congratulate ourselves on the fine weather. The Queen then went upstairs, and walked through the second banquetting hall, to show herself; after which she entered a small room where there was a throne, and there Her Majesty received the Address, which was read by the Recorder, and returned her answer. I always delight in hearing the Queen read or speak; her voice has such a clear and beautiful tone, and her enunciation is so correct and good. After the Address, she created the Lord Mayor (Sir William Magnay) a Baronet; and then Her Majesty retired with her ladies to a withdrawing-room, where we found the Duchess of Kent and the Duke of Cambridge. We waited a considerable time till the banquet was ready. The Queen sat at the top of the room, at a raised table, with the Prince at her right and the Duke of Cambridge at her left, and about ten other persons of the highest rank, including the French and Turkish Ambassadors and their wives. We sat at the top of the first table, with all the Ministers; and I was lucky enough to sit next my dear old friend Baron

Dedel, the Dutch Minister. I had a most entertaining luncheon, as he was as amusing and agreeable as ever.

The Queen returned to Buckingham Palace immediately after luncheon, and we got there by three o'clock. We came to Slough in Her Majesty's carriage, and afterwards dined with her. The Queen did not appear at all tired, and both she and the Prince were very much gratified by their reception and the way everything went off. I always prefer being in waiting when there are no visitors, as then we see so much more of the Queen; she asks after you and papa nearly every day.

Windsor Castle, October 30, 1844.—I am just come up to my room from a most agreeable and entertaining breakfast. Sir Robert Peel and Lord Ellenborough have been talking the whole time, telling us all sorts of funny and interesting anecdotes, and sending us all into fits of laughter. I hardly ever saw Sir Robert so well, or in such high spirits, and he was so amusing. In the first place, he told us that the other day, when the Queen went to the City, the Lord Mayor put on a huge pair of jack-boots over his shoes and stockings, to keep the mud off. Unfortunately, the boots were too tight; so when the Queen was approaching by no possibility could he get them off. One of the spurs caught in the fur trimming of an alderman's dress, and the Lord Mayor stood with one leg out whilst several men were tugging at the boot to try and get it off! In the meantime the Queen was coming nearer and nearer, and when she was only a few paces off the poor Lord Mayor was in an agony, with one boot off and the other on. At last, Sir Robert said, he got quite beside himself, and shouted out, 'For God's sake put my boot on again!'—(A boot! a boot! My mayoralty for a boot!)—and, sure enough, he only just got his boots on in time, and had to wear them till after the banquet, when he made one more successful attempt to divest himself of them; but the scene at Temple Bar must have been most truly ludicrous. Then Sir Robert told us he once dined at a large Lord Mayor's dinner at Guildhall, and sat next a famous Alderman Flower, whilst Mr. Canning sat on his other side; and he heard Flower remark to Canning, 'Mr. Canning, my Lord Ellenborough (the Lord Chief Justice) was a man of uncommon sagacity.' So Canning bowed assent, and said he believed he was; but asked what gave rise to the observation at that moment, upon which Alderman Flower answered, 'Why, sir, had he been here, he would have told me by a single glance of his eye which is the best of those five haunches of venison!'

This anecdote reminds me of a funny story I heard some years later. —— who was perfectly bald, but never wore a wig, was dining at the Lord Mayor's, when the aiguillette of one of the footmen's state liveries caught in the wig of his neighbour, and whisked it off. A waiter, seeing the wig on the floor, looked round for the baldest head, and, to his extreme disgust and annoyance, pitched it upon poor ——!

I was quite delighted when I heard yesterday that Lord Ellenborough was coming to Windsor. He remembered me perfectly, and I reminded him of our pleasant visit to Southam some years ago, and the beautiful bouquet of moss roses he gave me then. I cannot say his looks are improved by his stay in India; his hair is very grizzled, and his face not yellow, but red. He told me that though he was never ill there, he never felt well; but he went out determined to die rather than consult a doctor, as he had no confidence in any out there, and felt convinced they would kill him. Soon after his arrival at Calcutta he sent a medical man, at one o'clock, to a friend who was ill, and when he saw him at dinner-time he inquired how his patient was, and was told he had died at three; so from that moment Lord Ellenborough made up his mind to have nothing more to say to the faculty at Calcutta, and he actually went to Gwalior without any doctor on his staff.

Sir Robert and Lady Sale are coming here in a day or two; so I shall have seen many remarkable people this waiting. Lord Ellenborough told us one more funny story *à propos* of a Lord Mayor's dinner. The Duke of Wellington was called upon to propose the health of the Lady Mayoress, whom he had never set eyes on, and who happened to be a very plain, wizened little woman, when to his extreme surprise the Duke in his speech called her the model of her sex! After dinner he could not resist saying to the Duke, 'How could you call that ugly little creature the model of her sex?' The Duke laughed and said, 'Ha! ha! What the devil *could* I call her? I had never seen her before.'

Windsor Castle, October 31, 1844.—Sir Robert and Lady Sale arrived here yesterday, and I have been greatly interested in seeing and talking to them. Sir Robert took me in to dinner last night, and I conversed with Lady Sale all the evening; and she gave me many interesting particulars of her extraordinary life. She does not look like a heroine ; she is tall, and very thin, rather a plain woman, with a good open countenance, and her manners are very simple and unaffected. Sir Robert is stout, and has a comical expression ; he talks of cutting men down as if they were nettles. Lady Sale told me it was impossible to describe or conceive the fearful hardships they suffered in the dreadful and disastrous retreat from Cabul. When she left that place she wore a cloth habit, which got wet the first day, and from the intense cold became one sheet of solid ice, and for nine days she was never able to take it off. After Akhbar Khan took them prisoners, they were all huddled together, sometimes forty in a small hut, and packed so close she was obliged to ask whoever was next her to get up before she could turn. She was wounded in the arm the second day's march ; the ball went in just below her elbow, and came out at her wrist ; she showed me the large scars, and she had three other shots through her habit, but they did not wound her. A Dr. Price extracted the ball, and the first thing she saw the following day was his dead body lying stripped in one of the fearful defiles so graphically described by Lieut. Eyre, where our people were literally slaughtered like sheep, without being able to make the smallest resistance. Lady Sale's daughter, Mrs. Sturt, was confined during their imprisonment, and Lady Sale fortunately got hold of one of the chiefs in a good humour, who allowed her to have a little tiny room separated from the other prisoners, but without either air or light; and there her poor daughter was confined, without any medical assistance whatever; and, wonderful to relate, the baby, a girl, not only lived, but became a fine healthy child. They were often twenty-four hours without food, and Lady Sale said she remembered perfectly that after one of these long fasts they brought in a large dish of rice with sheep's tails in the middle, over which they poured a quantity of liquid fat, neither more nor less than tallow; and it was so filthy that, though she was nearly starving, she *could* not swallow it. They generally slept in the open air on the snow, the weather bitterly cold, but luckily there was no wind; they each had a sheepskin, upon one-half of which they slept, and the other half was wrapped round them. She was ten months in captivity, and besides the constant danger she was in of being murdered, she ran the most extraordinary risks from the difficulties and dangers of riding over uninhabited places where there were no roads, but frequent earthquakes. Once she was what they used to call ironing some clothes; that is to say, after their things had been dipped in a river, they spread them out on the top of the flat roofs of the houses, and patted them till they were dry. She was busily employed in this manner, when suddenly the roof she was on began to shake, and she had just time to jump off on to the roof of the next house when it fell in, she having left her daughter in the room beneath. She said it was impossible to describe the agony of that moment, for she thought her daughter must be killed; and she rushed down below, where, to her inexpressible relief, she found that, by God's mercy, Mrs. Sturt had just had time to escape.

Akhbar Khan pretended all the time to be her friend and protector, and he once asked her whether he could do anything for her; so she asked for writing materials, and said she wished to write to her husband, and hear from him. Akhbar Khan gave her permission, but said that all letters must pass through his hands, which they accordingly did; and sometimes he sent her a message to the effect that he had got letters for her, but was in a bad temper, and therefore he should not let her have them. He now and then tortured people who offended him by tearing off their nails one by one, feet as well as hands ; and he also tortured with the boot, like that which was used in the time of the Inquisition. Akhbar flattered himself that as long as Lady Sale was in his power Sir Robert would not fight against him, and he was much discomposed when he found that this fact only increased Sir Robert's energy and courage. Once when a messenger arrived announcing the defeat of some of his troops, Lady Sale was present, and Akhbar remarked a slight expression of pleasure and triumph on her countenance, so he asked her what she was laughing at. Of course she said nothing ; but he said he knew she was laughing at him, and that she was just as great a devil as her husband.

Sir Robert told me he never thought his wife would be sacrificed, because the Afghans will do anything for money, and he knew they considered her like a bale of valuable goods, which they were determined to make the most of. He heard that one man had great influence with Akhbar, so he sent for him and bribed him with 10,000 rupees to get his wife and daughter released. The man said he had no influence, but his mother had, for she had nursed Akhbar Khan, and in that country if the wet nurse takes hold of her foster child's beard, he is bound by the law of the land to grant her request, whatever it may be. When the Afghan saw the money he said he would try and do his best, and left the camp an hour after. He remained away a week, which Sir Robert considered a bad omen; and when he returned he said his mission had failed, for that Akhbar would sooner part with all his other prisoners than he would with Lady Sale, for he thought she was the only hold he had upon her devil of a husband!

The Queen sent for me when I had written thus far, and I have been with Her Majesty upwards of three hours. She has been sitting all the time—first to Gibson for her bust, and then to Thorburn, who is doing a beautiful miniature as a pendant to the one of the Prince you have so often heard me admire. It did surprise me to see the Queen's exemplary patience, for sitting such a number of hours must be very fatiguing, and a great bore; but I liked watching the progress of the work, and the Queen talked a great deal, and was very agreeable. I asked Her Majesty to let me see the album of the Eu drawings, given her by Louis Philippe, and she immediately sent for it. It is a splendid book; large folio, and rather difficult to handle; but some of the drawings are beautiful, and so very exact they are most interesting. I received my orders yesterday to attend the Queen to Burghley on the 12th.

Windsor Castle, November 5, 1844.—Such a beautiful statue arrived here yesterday from Rome, a full length figure of 'Penelope,' by Wyatt, standing in a pensive attitude, with one hand on her heart and the other holding a crook, with a fine dog looking up in her face. The drapery is exceedingly graceful, and the expression of her beautiful countenance very lovely but sad. The Queen is much pleased with it, and it is considered Wyatt's *chef d'œuvre.* The Duke and Duchess of Bedford, Lord and Lady Clarendon, and the Ashleys are here. The Duchess of Bedford has asked me to go to Woburn with the Normanbys whenever I like. She is very kind. Lord Clarendon is charming, and so very agreeable. We sat a long time at breakfast this morning, and he was so comical, he kept us all in roars of laughter. He has the quaintest, dryest, and cleverest way of saying sharp things. Yesterday they wished to see the Royal children; and as they are generally with the Queen when Her Majesty passes through the corridor after luncheon, Lady Portman asked Lady

Clarendon to wait a few minutes in the oak room till the Queen came; so Lady Clarendon told her lord not to go away, as they were to see the children; and he, not having heard the arrangement, said in the gravest manner: 'What! an audience through the keyhole; eh, Katty! how satisfactory!' Last night we were talking of the value of time and punctuality, and he remarked that Lady Clarendon had so little notion of either, that had it not been for him she would now have been in the year 1842; so that in point of fact he considered he had already added two years to her life since he married. This morning he has been telling us about their tour in Germany, which was most amusing.

Windsor Castle, November 7, 1844.—There was a household dinner yesterday, but at half-past nine the Queen sent for us to play, and we remained in her room till half-past eleven. Her Majesty and the Prince played a great many duets to us, and the Queen has lent us some of her books to look over. No one could be kinder or more amiable than Her Majesty has been, and I have seen so much more than usual of her this waiting, which makes such a difference; and this is the reason I always prefer being in waiting when none of the Queen's relations are staying here.

Windsor Castle, November 8, 1844.—We had such a gay evening last night, for after dinner the Queen began polkaing with Countess Wratislaw, and made her give a regular dancing lesson. We afterwards played at a new German game, and then another of my accomplishments was brought into play, for the Prince began spinning counters, so I took to spinning rings, which you know I am an adept at doing, and the Queen was delighted. It always entertains me to see the little things which amuse Her Majesty and the Prince, instead of their looking bored as people so often do in English society. The Queen supplied me with her different rings, and gave the history of each. One, a small enamel with a tiny diamond in the centre, the Prince gave her the first time he came to England, when he was sixteen. Another beautiful emerald serpent he gave her after they were engaged. The next, the Queen said, 'was my wedding ring,' which she has never taken off; and yesterday, when a cast was taken of her hand, Her Majesty was in an agony lest the ring should come off with the plaster.

Windsor Castle, November 9, 1844 (*the Prince of Wales' Birthday*).—I am just returned from such a pretty little review of the Guards and

Blues in honour of the Prince of Wales' birthday. It was such a lovely sight, for luckily the day was very bright and warm, like May. The Queen and Prince stood out with their three children whilst the troops marched past, presenting arms, and afterwards fired a *feu de joie.* The children behaved so well, and I am sure the soldiers must have been pleased at getting such a good view of them, as they marched by quite close. The Princess Royal was the only one who appeared a little frightened at the firing, and towards the end, when the band struck up 'God save the Queen,' she thought, poor child, that it was going to begin again, so she put her little hands up to her ears, which shocked the Queen dreadfully. I never did see such good children, even little Princess Alice stood all the time and never moved—the group was a very pretty sight.

Admiral Sir William Parker came here yesterday. He is just come home from China, and has been giving us an entertaining account of the Chinese. He spoke in such very high terms of George Wellesley, and said he considered him not only one of the best and most honourable officers, but one of the best men in the navy, so he could not conceive why he had not been promoted long ago. Sir William wrote to Lord Haddington about him, but added he did not like to press the point too much for fear people should think he did so on account of George Wellesley being a nephew of the Duke of Wellington; so, so far from this being any advantage to him, it was rather the contrary. Last night the Queen asked me whether I could dance a reel, and though the other ladies could not, we danced one *con amore*. It was very amusing, and made the Queen laugh heartily. I never remember seeing Her Majesty in such high spirits; she told us a great deal about her visit to Scotland and Blair Athol, which she evidently delights in; indeed, she says there is nothing like the Highlands. She was out deer-stalking one day for nine hours, not allowed to speak above a whisper, and had to hide among the rocks and heather for fear of disturbing the herd. It was so interesting to hear Her Majesty describe it all herself, and say how much she enjoyed it.

We had another long interview with the Queen and the Royal children in the corridor; the Prince of Wales was dressed in a kilt, and looked so pretty. He is really a beautiful boy, with such a sweet expression in his large eyes. You would have laughed at seeing me teaching the Queen and Princess Royal how to make a little stuffed mouse run over their hands as if it were alive.

Buckingham Palace, November 12, 1844.—The servants left this morning at 5 A.M., and there was a question whether we should get up at four or do without our maids and things; so like a true Liddell I preferred three hours more bed to my dressing-box, and the housemaid helped me to dress. We got back from Drury Lane at eleven last night. We saw Auber's Opera of the Siren, and some of the music is pretty. The fair maid of Ghent was the ballet, and there was a famous danseuse Dumélatre. Mr. Bunn very improperly, and against orders, gave out that the Queen intended honouring the theatre with her presence; so there was a very full house, and a tremendous row for about ten minutes because Her Majesty declined going forward. The audience would not allow the opera to go on, so at last the National Anthem was played, and the Queen stood up and showed herself. Her Majesty was immensely cheered, and though the manager was to blame, it is right and natural that people should wish to see, and as they think, do honour to their Sovereign, and so one does not like their loyalty to be repressed.

I had such a nice *tête-à-tête* drive with the Queen yesterday to Kensington and Gloucester

House. The dear old Duchess called me in and was so kind. She asked affectionately after you and my father, and spoke to the Queen in the highest terms of my brother Augustus Liddell.

Burghley, Tuesday, November 12, 1844.—We had a very prosperous journey here, though the weather was dull and wet, but very mild. We reached Weedon at twelve and Northampton about half-past twelve. There the reception was beautiful; a multitude of people, but on the whole a well-behaved and very enthusiastic mob. The streets were decorated with flags and banners, there were a great many triumphal arches and evergreens everywhere, and the yeomanry and tenants met us eight or ten miles from this place, and escorted Her Majesty—such an immense body of them, even larger than at Belvoir last year. It was getting dark when we arrived, but I could just see the outline of this beautiful mansion, the interior of which is magnificent. We only passed through the drawing-room, as the Queen retired to her apartment immediately, so I just saw the Duchess of Bedford, Lady Willoughby, and Lady Charles Wellesley. I have got a lovely little room next Lady Portman's, and close to the Queen's rooms. All fitted up with blue satin and quantities of pictures. The view of the bridge, which is illuminated, is so pretty.

Burghley, November 13, 1844.—I have been drawing to-day, as the Queen desired me to try and sketch the inner Court, but it is a difficult architectural drawing, which requires real care and precision, and I fear I shall not have time to make anything of it. I sat between Sir Robert Peel and Lord Stanley at dinner, and have been talking to the latter all the evening—he is so very entertaining. It rained nearly all day, so we could not go out, but there is so much to be seen inside the house, and such pictures. It is really a magnificent place. Lord Exeter has got the ancient patent, and it is spelt Burghley.

Burghley, Thursday, November 14, 1844.—The weather to-day has been very bright and fine. We went out in an open carriage after luncheon, and the Queen drove twice through Stamford. The old town looked so bright and pretty, with banners and flags waving out of every window. There was a large concourse of people, and they behaved very well. I was in the second carriage with Sir Robert Peel (who was heartily cheered), Lord de la Warr, and Lady Thomas Cecil. After leaving Stamford we drove to Lord Exeter's paddocks to see his racehorses, and a beautiful old house Wodrop, which was built at the same date as this, but is now in ruins. Lord Exeter told us it was originally built for the family to go to once every year whilst Burghley was being swept! When the Queen came back from driving she went to the front of the house, and planted an oak tree, and Prince Albert planted a lime. There is to be a great ball to-night, to which all the neighbours for miles round are invited, and some are coming above forty miles! Yesterday, when the Queen went through the house, we had to pass through ——'s room, and lo! his best wig and whiskers were put out on a block on the drawers. Luckily, —— was not with us, it was such a funny incident.

We are to leave this a quarter before nine to-morrow, and hope to arrive at Windsor about six. The visit has gone off very well, and I think the Queen has enjoyed it very much. I like accompanying Her Majesty on these occasions, and they are interesting to look back to.

Windsor Castle, Saturday, November 16, 1844. —We arrived here about seven o'clock yesterday, having had a prosperous, though rather a long day's journey. We left Burghley at half-past nine, but the roads were so heavy and the poor horses so knocked up with the quantity of work they have had lately, that the Queen had to slacken the speed of her horses, as the other carriages could not keep up; and as it was we waited some time for Her Majesty's dressers at Weedon, since the Queen objected to leaving them and all her things to follow by a later train. There was again a very large concourse of people at Northampton, but I do not think the crowd was so great as it was last Tuesday. We passed Boughton, which seems an ugly, though very large house; the great peculiarity of the place is the immense extent of avenues in all directions. We were told there are nearly one hundred miles of avenue, and one of the owners of the place bought just enough land to make them without in the least caring to have the property on either side. But this gives the appearance of great extent, and the trees are now very fine; but the country we passed through was flat and uninteresting. We saw one very pretty old cross like the one at Waltham, which marks the spot where Queen Eleanor's body rested. The ball at Burghley was rather dull. The Queen did not dance herself, but looked pleased and gracious, and most of the evening the guests passed by as they do at a drawing-room. I did not know many people, but danced with Lord Burghley, Mr. Clive, and Lord Lovaine, and was engaged to do so with Lord Granby and Lord Brooke, but the Queen went to supper at twelve; and though she asked me whether I should like to return to the ball-room after it, I preferred going to bed, as I had to get up so very early next morning, and I had had quite enough standing! Lord Lovaine took me in to dinner last night, and I thought him very clever and agreeable. Generally speaking, I have only seen the Cabinet Ministers to speak to, so very soon I shall not condescend to speak to any one who is not a Prime Minister; and as I know you are anxious about seeing some young men at Ravensworth, I have invited Sir Robert Peel, Lord Stanley, and Sir James Graham to come there, so I hope you will be satisfied!

Windsor Castle, November 19, 1844.—We had another charming evening with the Queen and Prince last night in their private apartment, and played till eleven o'clock.

These practices must be very improving, and it is fortunate that Matilda Paget and I read music with facility; for we generally have to play overtures and classical pieces at sight. Last night we played Beethoven's 'Septuor;' and the Queen observed it was quite a relief to find when we came to the last bar that we were all playing together, for had any of us gone wrong it would have been rather difficult to find one's place again! I enjoy nothing so much as seeing the Queen in that nice quiet way, and I often wish that those who don't know Her Majesty could see how kind and gracious she is when she is perfectly at her ease, and able to throw off the restraint and form which must and ought to be observed when she is in public.

CHAPTER VI.

My Marriage—Letter from the Queen—Departure for Russia—Hamburg, Lubeck; arrival at St. Petersburg—Society—My Presentation at Tzarskoe Selo—Death of my Mother, Lady Ravensworth—Bear Shooting; Accident to the Hon. Henry Elliot—Anecdotes.

THE Hon. John Arthur Douglas Bloomfield, who was then Envoy Extraordinary and Minister Plenipotentiary at the Court of St. Petersburg, was at home on leave. I had met him two years previously at Belvoir; but had almost forgotten him, when one day he came to call at Percy's Cross. My mother was out, and I was sitting in my own room, when I got a message from my father desiring me to come down-stairs.

I found him talking to a gentleman, and when I entered he said to me, 'Georgy, don't you recollect Mr. Bloomfield?' My father was anxious to finish some letters for the post, and desired me to show Mr. Bloomfield the garden; so we took a walk together, and from that moment his intentions were very evident, as he took every opportunity of meeting me and showing me attention. Our marriage was settled on July 26, just after I had resigned my appointment at Court, in consequence of my dear mother's delicate state of health, not having then the least idea of marriage. I wrote to the Queen to announce my engagement to Mr. Bloomfield, and received the following kind letter of congratulation from her Majesty :—

'Osborne, July 29, 1845.

'My dearest Georgiana,—I received this morning your kind letter announcing your marriage with Mr. Bloomfield, which has surprised us most agreeably. I do not think you guilty of any inconsistency, and we only hope you will be *as* happy through a long life as *we are*; I *cannot* wish you *more* than this. I highly approve your choice, having a high opinion of Mr. Bloomfield; and I shall be much pleased to have, as the wife of my representative at St. Petersburg, a person who has been about me, whom I am so partial to, and who I am sure will perform the duties of her position extremely well. I pity you much for the painful separation from Mr. Bloomfield to which you will be subjected.

Once more repeating our sincere wishes for your happiness, and with our kind regards to your parents, who we hope are better,

'Believe me,

'Always yours affectionately,

'VICTORIA R.'

My engagement to the only son of one of their oldest and most attached friends gave my parents the greatest satisfaction, and my dear mother would not hear of the marriage being postponed, or of my failing in what she considered my first duty—viz., accompanying my husband, who was compelled to return to St. Petersburg. Had I been aware of my dear mother's danger, nothing would have induced me to leave her; but the doctor held out hopes, which, alas! proved delusive, of her living a considerable time, so I was married at Lamesley Church, Co. Durham, on September 4, by my brother Robert; and we spent our honeymoon at Whitburne Hall. On the 11th we returned to Ravensworth, and stayed there till the 16th, when we went to Kingscote, Beckett, Woolwich, and Windsor, where we took leave of the Queen previously to going to Russia. Thursday, October 2, we sailed on board the 'Lightning' for Hamburg. Lord Bloomfield,

Mr. Woolwych Whitmore, Miss Ellen Sheppard, and the Rev. James Connolly, Lord Bloomfield's chaplain, accompanied us to Gravesend, where they took leave of us; and I was fairly launched on the voyage of life. We reached the Nore at 6 P.M., where we saw the 'Éclair,' which was then in quarantine, with the yellow-fever on board. The wind was fair, and the sea perfectly calm. On Friday, the 3rd, we made the Texel, and Saturday morning, at 10 A.M., we reached Cuxhaven, and arrived at Hamburg at five that afternoon.

The banks of the Elbe are flat and uninteresting, till within about twelve miles of Hamburg, where the left bank rises, and is prettily covered with villas and gardens belonging to the rich merchants, who reside there during the summer months. We were struck with the amazing quantity of wild fowl which frequent the marshy islets on the Elbe. When we landed at Hamburg, we went straight to call on Colonel Hodges, the British Chargé d'Affaires, who accompanied us to Streit's Hotel, where he had taken rooms for us. Sunday, the 5th, we attended the English church, walked about the town, and dined with Colonel Hodges, where we met two old colleagues of my husband's, M. Kaiserfeldt, the Austrian Minister, and M. Bille, the Danish Minister. On Monday we went to some excellent shops, and drove in the afternoon, with Colonel Hodges and M. de Bille, to a famous garden about five miles out of the town, belonging to a Mr. Booth, a Scotchman, who is celebrated for his fine collection of orchids. Among other hot-house plants, I particularly remarked the *Aphelandra aurantiaca*, the *Diplodonia crassinoda*, the Chlorodendron, and a splendid scarlet passion-flower, called *Ratzimosa*. Tuesday was a very wet day; but we took a walk, and dined with Colonel Hodges, where we met Lord Brooke and Mr. Repton (who had just returned from a tour in Sweden and Norway), M. and Madame Wrangel, Mr. and Mrs. Swaine, M. Bacherach (a Russian), M. Bille, and M. Kaiserfeldt.

Colonel Hodges was intimate with Lord and Lady Clanricarde. One year he had arrived in England from Hamburg, when he met Lady Clanricarde out driving. She stopped her carriage to speak to him, and when he inquired after her husband Lady Clanricarde pointed upwards, and said, 'He is there!' Colonel Hodges fancied for a moment that she meant Lord Clanricarde was dead; but, raising his eyes, he saw a balloon just passing over their heads at that moment, which contained Lord Clanricarde!

Wednesday and Thursday were very wet. I sketched one of the Hamburg flower-girls, whose dress was exceedingly picturesque, and consisted of a large, round straw hat, with a tight black cap underneath fitting close to the head, with two large bows and black ribbons behind; an embroidered jacket, with a plain cloth one over it adorned with silver buckles, and a little red trimming; a dark petticoat, an apron, bright blue or purple stockings, and black velvet shoes.

Friday, October 10.—We left Hamburg at 10 A.M., and posted to Lubeck, about forty-five miles, where we arrived at three. It never ceased raining the whole day; but we nevertheless visited the two principal churches, the Dom and the Maria Kirche—both very interesting, though the finest monuments are in the latter—and we saw Holbein's curious picture of the 'Dance of Death.' We also saw a beautiful old room in the Town Hall, the walls of which were entirely covered with carvings in wood and ivory. It was made early in the sixteenth century, by one of the Lubeck merchants, and is considered one of the curiosities of the place.

Sunday, October 12.—We attended divine service at the Maria Kirche, and I was much struck with the eloquence and fervour of the preacher. His dress reminded me of the pictures of the Reformers; he wore a black gown and very large ruffles. The organ was fine, and the singing would have been tolerably good, but for one old man, who had a most discordant voice, and screeched dreadfully out of tune at the top of his voice. The service consisted of two Psalms, then the blessing, Lord's prayer, and sermon; after which there were several short extempore prayers, for different members of the congregation then assembled, for a woman after childbirth, for a minister about to be ordained, and for two ships which had left the harbour. Another Psalm was sung, and then the officiating minister went to the Communion-table, and chanted something we could not follow, after which the service ended. The Amens were very impressive, and the sermon, from our own Epistle for the day—the tenth verse of the sixth chapter of Ephesians—very good. It dwelt upon the importance of making religion part and parcel of life; beginning from the moment of our being made members of Christ's Church at our baptism, it should grow with our growth, and strengthen with our strength. If fostered in our childhood by our parents, when we are separated from them and left, perhaps, without any earthly guide, we should feel that we have a Father in heaven who has promised to watch over and protect those who flee to him for succour, and enable those who trust in him to 'fight manfully under his banner against sin, the world, the flesh, and the devil.'

After church we took a long walk round the environs of the town, which are very pretty. We began to feel anxious at the non-arrival of the 'Lightning,' which went round the Skaw, and ought to have reached Travemünde on Thursday.

Monday, October 13.—The weather was fine. We walked to the borders of the lake, and witnessed a glorious sunset. The town, with its fine churches and picturesque spires, stood out in rich purple against a golden sky; every tower was reflected as in a mirror on the still waters of the lake—not a breath of wind disturbed them; and the scene was so very beautiful we both gazed on it for some time in speechless admiration.

Tuesday, October 14.—We could hear nothing of our ship. The autumn was advancing; and, as my husband was in a hurry to return to his post, he decided that we must continue our voyage to St. Petersburg in the 'Naslednik,' the ordinary passenger boat between Travemünde and Cronstadt. All the best cabins were taken;

ACADEMIE DES BEAUX-ARTS, ST. PETERSBURG.

so I had to content myself with a very horrid second-class cabin; and we sailed at 3.30 P.M.

The dirt, discomfort, and wretchedness exceeded all description; but, fortunately, the weather was bright and calm, and the wind fair.

Saturday, October 18.—We anchored at Cronstadt a little before 8 A.M., and, thanks to one of our fellow-passengers, Mr. Alexander Baird, who lent us one of his steamers—the 'Alexander'—we were enabled to leave the 'Naslednik' before the other passengers, and reached St. Petersburg before one o'clock. My first impressions of the Neva were very unfavourable. The weather was cold, and the low banks looked wintry, with a sprinkling of snow. I was much struck by the curious appearance of the boatmen on the various boats we passed, all dressed in their sheepskins, fur caps, and enormous tan fingerless gloves. I thought they looked very savage; great was my delight and thankfulness when we reached our house, Dom Stroukoff, on the English Quay. Mr. Buchanan, the Secretary of Legation, received us, and we found everything prepared, as the servants had been expecting us for some days.

In the afternoon I took my first drive round the town. I had left all my things—trousseau, jewels, and books—on board the 'Lightning,' which had not arrived; so I was forced to buy myself a few articles of dress. I was much struck with the town, especially the Winter Palace, Admiralty Place, and the churches; their size is very grand, and the costumes of the watchmen and moujiks amused me very much. The pavement was atrocious, and shook me to pieces; it was enough to break, not only every spring of one's carriage, but every bone in one's body.

Sunday and Monday passed without any tidings of our ship, and we began to get seriously anxious about her safety; but on Tuesday my husband rushed into my room with the welcome news that the Cronstadt boat had arrived, with the English flag flying from the mast-head—a sign that an English man-of-war had arrived at Cronstadt, and, as we knew no other frigate was expected, we felt sure our ship was come. We immediately sent down to the quay, and were delighted to see our kind captain, Mr. Petley, and our poor English housemaid, who had been left on board. We almost felt as if they had risen from the dead! They had an awful storm twenty hours after they sailed from Hamburg, which lasted for five days without intermission, during which the ship had to lie before the wind. The boat was damaged; there was a large hole in the boiler; and, unfortunately, the sea broke into the fresh water tanks, which had been left uncovered when the storm began; so for nearly five days the crew were without fresh water, and my poor housemaid was reduced to drinking some I had left in a stone foot-warmer. She suffered dreadfully, and said she never expected to see land again, but had quite made up her mind that the vessel would go down. She declared she would rather be drowned than undergo another week of such suffering. Some of the sailors and the stewardess, who had gone on shore on the Sunday at Hamburg to amuse themselves, reproached themselves bitterly, and kept saying the storm was a judgment upon them for having so misspent the Lord's Day; so Mary said it had been a comfort to her in that dreadful moment to think she had not been of the party. After the storm subsided the captain had to put in to Egesund, a small Norwegian port, where he got some fresh water and provisions. As no steamers ever went there, the inhabitants flocked in great numbers to see the 'Lightning,' which reached Travemünde just sixteen hours after we had left it. All our goods and chattels arrived safely, and not much the worse, except that some of my books were stained with the salt water.

My diplomatic colleagues were Countess Bray *née* Dentice, the wife of the Bavarian Minister and the Doyenne of the Corps Diplomatique, Baroness Seebach *née* Nesselrode, Madame de Rantzau, and Countess de Rayneval *née* Bertin de Vaux, a very clever, agreeable, and accomplished young woman, and a good musician. I made the acquaintance of Countess Woronzow Daschkow *née* Narischkine, Countess Sophie Bobrinsky *née* Zamailoff, who afterwards became my dearest friend, and who was certainly one of the most charming women I ever had the good fortune of knowing. She was an intimate friend of the Empress, and saw her constantly, but would never accept any official position at Court after her marriage, though she had been Maid of Honour to the Empress Elizabeth, the wife of the Emperor Alexander. Count Bobrinsky was a grandson of the Empress Katherine, his grandfather having been one of her favourites, and Count Alexis Bobrinsky bore a strong resemblance to the busts of the Empress. The L—— house on the quay was one of the finest at St. Petersburg, and was full of works of art and a fine collection of Egyptian curiosities. The L——'s had only one son, and he was an inveterate gambler. His father remonstrated with him, and after paying his gambling debts several times declared he would never do so again. Not long after the young man came and told him he had lost another large sum of money, and that he had made up his mind to blow his brains out unless it was paid. His father thinking this was merely an idle threat, persisted in his resolution, and so the young man went up to his room and shot himself, to the dismay and despair of his unfortunate parents.

Madame L —— was a singular character. She gave very pleasant dinners, and we frequently dined at her house. After her death her son-in-law told me there was a dark room she kept the key of, into which no one had been allowed to enter for thirty years, in which she was in the habit of hoarding all kinds of things. After a dinner party she collected the candle ends, bonbons, &c. : she kept all the notes and letters she ever received, and very often put rouble notes of large value into them. She fancied she was so poor, she sometimes gave her grandchildren's nurse a few roubles to buy gloves, stockings, or a pocket handkerchief, whilst she had dozens of the most beautiful ones sent from Paris, which were all found tied up with the coloured ribbons they were sent in. There were three hundred pieces of silks for dresses, seventy pairs of stays, and in one corner of this den there was a crumpled old bandbox, which contained a magnificent parure of emeralds worth many thousands!

The Woronzow Daschkow's house was one of the finest and most beautifully furnished at St. Petersburg. At the small parties only the rooms on the first floor were opened. The walls and furniture were covered with the richest crimson damask, with velvet *portières* of the same colour; but I was struck by the apparent want of occupation, books, etc., in all the rooms; and when I was received in the morning I generally found the lady of the house sitting in a very dark room in a sort of *bosquet* of Oriental plants or ivy, evidently sitting up for company. The Russian ladies never appeared to occupy themselves, and their chief interest was the theatre; their first question invariably was, what plays I had seen. A ball at Countess Levaschoff's was brilliantly lighted, and the rooms opened upon a beautiful conservatory, where a fountain was playing.

Baron Seebach took us to the best fur-shop in the Gastinadvor, or Bazaar. The old merchant made many bows and protestations of friendship, and showed us some magnificent fur, among the rest a lining of black fox worth 10,000 roubles. At that time the rouble was worth

3*s*. 2*d*. My husband gave me a handsome blue fox lining and sable collar, a beautiful sable boa and muff. He had to submit to an embrace from the merchant; but we were surprised on reaching home to find that the fur had been changed for some one-third less in value. We immediately sent to remonstrate, and our messenger returned with the fur we had chosen, and said it was a mistake; but no doubt one the merchant would gladly have profited by.

Monday, November 3.—The day was fine, so I took my first drive to the Islands. At this season they looked very wretched, like a succession of deserted tea gardens, and the roads were dreadful. On another day we drove to the Smolna convent. The church is an immense size, and the columns are all of white marble. Sir James Wylie dined with us. He was a remarkable man and quite a character; he was the Emperor Alexander's doctor, and always attended him throughout all his campaigns, and remained with him till he died. He told me he was the first person who saw the Emperor Paul after he was murdered, as he was sent for to embalm the body, and make it presentable. It is the custom in Russia for the bodies of members of the Imperial family to lie in state for some days previous to interment, and people flock in great numbers to see the corpse of a Czar, and kiss the hand.

Wednesday, November 12.—The ice began coming down the river in small quantities, and the bridges were removed. We were rather amused at hearing that a party had been invited to dine with the Grand Duke Michael, to eat some English mutton, which is considered a great delicacy at St. Petersburg. This turned out to be a poor sheep my father sent me, which broke its leg on the voyage from England, and had to be killed immediately; but which we could not use because the meat was bad, so it was sold by our cook to the Grand Duke's, as a great favour, but of course when the meat came to table it was not eatable!

I had a long conversation with Dr. Rogers about the state of the poor in Russia. Where the serfs had good masters, they were perhaps better off than the poor in England, but when they were oppressed they had no redress; for even if they applied to the authorities the owner, by dint of bribery, generally got a decision in his favour, and then the unfortunate serf and his family underwent such persecution, that rather than run the risk of offending their owner, they preferred submitting to any hardship. In the southern provinces they suffered great privation, and Dr. Rogers said he had frequently seen them gather crab apples, which they dried, pounded, and mixed with a small quantity of meal. I heard a story, which I believe to be quite true, which gives a sad picture of the serf in Russia. A nobleman had two sons, the eldest legitimate, the youngest illegitimate; but he greatly preferred the latter, and gave him a very good education. He had great talent as an artist, and was getting on very well, when his father died, and he then became the property of his elder brother, who hated him ; so he sent for him and told him he must leave St. Petersburg, and return to the plough in the interior of Russia. The wretched man in despair declared this would be his utter ruin, and that he was willing to pay any poll-tax his brother liked to impose upon him, if he might only be allowed to remain at St. Petersburg, and carry on his profession ; but the elder brother was inexorable, and said he did not want his money but his ruin, as he hated him, and so he had to go. Surely no human being ought to have such unlimited power over the life and fortunes of a fellow-creature.

There were a number of hospitals at St. Petersburg and Moscow, which were tolerably well managed, but in the provinces the poor were very badly off from the want of medical aid, and suffered very much from a low typhus fever.

November 16.—Having been summoned to Tzarskoe Selo, we left home at twelve o'clock in our chariot with four horses abreast, and reached Tzarskoe Selo at two, the distance being about twenty versts (a verst is three-quarters of a mile). The road, which is flat, is very uninteresting, but wide and tolerably good, with rows of trees on each side. We passed one pretty village belonging to the Emperor. The houses were all built of wood, with gable ends and balconies, and all had double windows. A peasant's house in Russia is called an Isba. On arriving at the Palace, we were immediately shown to our apartments, which were on the second floor—handsome as to size, but wretchedly furnished, with just a bare table, a few chairs, and a very stiff uncomfortable sofa placed against the wall There were three smaller rooms, and although we had been offered beds we were evidently not expected to accept the offer, as there was only one small single bed in the ante-room. By asking we succeeded in getting wash-hand stands. We called on Madame Baranoff, the lady-in-waiting, and then dressed for dinner. We were taken across the great Court in a Court carriage, and conducted to the Imperial apartments, where I met my Portuguese colleague, Madame Correa, who was also to be presented. The Emperor Nicholas and the Empress were at that time spending the winter at Palermo for the Empress' health, which was very delicate. Presently the Czarewna, or Grand Duchesse Héritière, came in, and I was presented to her, then to her husband, the Czarewitch, the Grand Duchess Marie, and her husband, the Duc de Leuchtenberg, and Prince Alexander of Hesse, the Czarewna's brother. Immediately after my presentation we went in to dinner, and I followed the Imperial family, and sat next the Grand Maréchal de la Cour. There was a large Court, I should say about a hundred and fifty or two hundred people. I sat opposite the Czarewitch, and a band played during dinner. After dinner we adjourned for a short time to the drawing-room, where I made the acquaintance of two curious old ladies, Madame Apraxine and Princess Dolgorouky, who had been maids of honour to the Empress Katherine, and accompanied her on her journey to the Crimea. They wore a number of decorations on their left shoulder. There were four maids of honour in waiting; they wear the Imperial cypher in diamonds on a blue ribbon. A little before six we returned to our rooms, where I was glad to rest till nine, when having changed my dress, we returned to the Imperial apartment, and were conducted to a small theatre belonging to the Palace, where two French plays were acted. Mademoiselle Plessis, who was making a great sensation at St. Petersburg at this period, was the chief attraction. She was a fine actress, and reminded me a little of Mademoiselle Mars; but she was badly supported, and I did not admire either of the plays, which were 'Quand l'amour s'en va,' and 'Rodolph; ou Frère et Sœur.' After the theatre, supper was served at a number of little round tables, and I was placed at the Czarewna's table; the Czarewitch moved about, and spoke to the assembled guests. As soon as supper was over we took leave, and returned to St. Petersburg, which we reached about three o'clock A.M. Tzarskoe Selo is a fine Palace, the rooms occupied by the Imperial family are the same as those the Empress Katherine lived in, and are exactly in the same state as they were in her reign. The parquet was inlaid with mother of pearl, and very beautiful; and I was struck by some very fine specimens of amber. We saw the Czarewitch's children, a nice little boy of about two years old, and his sisters. They were attended by English nurses. These are greatly preferred in Russia, and are generally bribed by the Russians to enter their service. A lady told me that a nurse who lived with her three years left to go to Princess B——, who gave her 70*l.* per annum, besides quantities of presents; and one day when my informant was calling on the Princess, the nurse sent in to say she wished to have the carriage and four to take the child an airing! This request was immediately acceded to, and she was met walking down the great staircase attended by a footman!

Madame R—— was married in the first instance to Prince ——, and after her marriage she informed him that M. de R—— was desperately in love with her, and that if he (her husband) would consent to a divorce, she would make him a handsome allowance. They consequently made an amicable arrangement on these terms; she continued to be very good friends with her first husband, but married his rival!

Dining at the N——'s, I was rather surprised at the loud and eager way conversation was carried on at dinner. Parties were divided as to the merits of Pauline Garcia, the *prima donna* at the Italian Opera, and another artiste; the disputes which took place were quite ludicrous. I was talking with one of my colleagues, who told me she lived in a flat, and was astonished to find one morning that her stair carpet had been carried off in the night. The brass bars which fastened it down were scattered about, and the thief succeeded in carrying off his prize without being discovered. Whilst Lord Clanricarde was Ambassador, all his silver mounted harness was stolen. I was told that Christmas and Easter are the favourite seasons for stealing, as it is usual to make presents then, and consequently servants 'rob Peter to pay Paul,' and rob their masters, not so much for their own profit, as for that of their friends.

And now occurred the most painful event in my hitherto happy and prosperous life! My beloved mother, who had long been in failing health, died at Ravensworth Castle on November 22. I draw a veil over the intense grief this sad loss caused my dear father and all her children; but now, after the expiration of thirty-six years, I can truly say the death of such a wife and mother caused a blank in our family which has never been filled up, and as days and years roll by, we have realised more and more how irreparable was the loss of one of the most devoted and affectionate of mothers, and the best of women.

Friday, December 21.—We were alarmed at the smell of fire in my sitting-room, and on taking up the grate we found that a cowhide, which was always placed under the grate by way of precaution, was smouldering. The horrible smell it caused gave us warning, and probably but for this the house would have been in a blaze. One night, soon after my arrival at St. Petersburg, I was awakened by the fortress guns firing. I did not know what this meant, so I asked my husband, who said, 'Oh! it is nothing—only an inundation.' As my only idea of an inundation was the terrible one I had read of in the year 1826, I was much alarmed, and suggested that we had better get up and prepare for the consequences; but was relieved at hearing that the guns were always fired whenever the Neva rose above the usual level. The second time they fire it is to warn people to remove their horses and cattle from the stables in the low parts of the town; the third time the inhabitants prepare for the worst, and lay in a supply of food. Almost every year the cellars of the houses on the quays are more or less flooded. My friend, Countess Bobrinsky, who lived on one of the canals at the back of the English quay, told me that during the great inundation in 1826, the *débris* cast against her house reached as high as the first floor, and that no less than eighteen bodies were removed from them when the flood abated. The cellars of the houses at St. Petersburg were frequently flooded during the winter, and the poor people who lived in them suffered greatly from typhus and other diseases caused by damp. The houses are built upon piles, and I was told that when the double windows are taken out in the summer they are numbered, but have generally to be refitted in the autumn, as the window frames have altered in shape! The quays are granite and very fine, but partly from the bad foundation and partly from the action of the frost, the stones shift and are not exactly in place. During the severe frost my veil was frequently a sheet of solid ice, the horse and sledge drivers are covered with rime, and the snow is so crisp that it flies like dust and crunches under one's feet. Carriage wheels will scarcely turn. One day I went to write my name down on the Grand Duchess of Oldenburg, and though my carriage was closed, and warmed with a hot bottle, the ink froze in my pen before I could write my name. That same day M. de H—— was skating in front of our windows, but had to walk home a short distance. He got very warm skating, but cooled walking, and when he got to his house his hat was frozen to his head, and he could not take it off!

The servants when I went to Russia were all

serfs. Some of them paid as much as two hundred roubles per annum poll-tax to their owners. The moujiks lived altogether apart from the foreign servants; in our house they had a small *entre sol*, which they kept excessively hot, never admitting a breath of fresh air during the winter, but they went out into the open air when there were many degrees of cold. The moujiks' rooms were never furnished, and I believe they slept on the floor wrapped up in their sheepskins. Their food consisted of cabbage, frozen fish, dried mushrooms, or rather toad-stools, called gribuï, stale eggs, and very bad oil. They mix these ingredients together in a pot and boil them, and this mess they greatly preferred to good food. When Lord Stuart de Rothesay was Ambassador, he wished to feed his moujiks like his other servants, but they declined eating the food the cook prepared for them. They wore a red shirt, loose cotton trowsers, boots outside their trowsers, a jacket and an apron, and they never undressed except once a week when they went to their bath, which was described to me as a large sort of flat oven, which is heated as much as possible, and then water is thrown over it, which causes a great steam. There are stages above this oven at various heights on which the bathers sit. The heat is intense, and causes profuse perspiration; but people will remain in it for twenty or twenty-five minutes, and then go out to the pump in the yard, where they pump on each other. This relieves the oppression in the head caused by the vapour, which often produces determination of blood to the head. Quite young children undergo this severe ordeal, though it frequently kills them.

It is curious how little the Russian minds the sudden transfer from intense heat to intense cold. A coachman will leave his room, which is unbearably hot, and sit on his coach-box for hours with impunity. The postillions, young lads, often go to sleep on their horses, and are sometimes frozen to death, but this generally happened after drinking spirits. Most of our moujiks could read and write, but were very ignorant and superstitious; they always crossed themselves whenever they passed a church, and observed the Lent and Advent fasts most strictly. During these they never touched animal food, not even milk, eggs or butter. Our footman, Foky, was a very good man, and always grew ostensibly thinner during these fasts; the last week before Easter his stockings quite bagged on his poor shrunken legs. I frequently found him in my ante-room reading the Bible in Slavonic, but I believe he was better than most Russian servants, and he certainly was a very honest, respectable man. One day our Maître d'Hôtel came to me in despair, begging me to go and see the pantry and still-room, which were alive with bugs. Our under butler had married, and instead of staying at home to look after the plate, took himself off after our dinner, so our Maître d'Hôtel, without telling us, desired one of the moujiks to sleep in the pantry, and the result was what I have described above. When we went to evening parties our servants waited for us in the entrance halls, which were warmed. I seldom came home without finding two or three bugs upon me. Our coachman wore a caftan and a red sash, which was made of several rolls of scarlet cashmere. When this was worn out, he brought it to show our Maître d'Hôtel, and it was generally found to be full of vermin, though to look at him one would have thought our coachman one of the smartest men in St. Petersburg.

January 3, 1846.—I drove to the frozen meat market, which was a very curious sight. The animals, oxen, pigs, calves, sheep, poultry and game were all heaped one above the other, and presented a ghastly appearance. They are sold in immense quantities, and one meets sledges full all over the town; and sometimes a soldier is seen with a sheep on his back. The meat and poultry are killed when winter commences, and sent up from the country in a frozen state; and they are allowed to remain so until required for use, when the meat is unfrozen by being soaked in cold water; it is then perfectly good, though rather tasteless, but if cooked before being properly unfrozen it is very bad. From the frozen market we drove for the first time across the Neva to the Fortress, and visited the Church of St. Peter and St. Paul, where the Imperial family are buried. Their stone coffins are covered with black velvet palls bearing the initials of the deceased. The Church is handsome, and kept warm; a lamp burns at each of the various altars, and there is a large collection of the Standards which have been taken in battle. The walls on one side of the Fortress are washed by the Neva. It is the State prison, and a most dismal-looking place.

The Hon. Henry Elliot, Lord Minto's second son, who was Second Attaché at the Legation, had a narrow escape while bear shooting. Whilst separated from his companions he met a very large brown bear, and waited till the animal was only three yards off before he fired. The bear was wounded, but not killed, and Mr. Elliot had only time to drop his gun and receive him on a spear, with which a peasant had fortunately provided him, when the bear came upon him. The bear was mortally wounded, but the snow was so deep Mr. Elliot lost his balance, and fell on his back with the bear over him. He managed, however, to keep hold of the spear with his right hand, and with his left defended his head, which is what a bear always tries to attack first. The bear bit Mr. Elliot's left hand and arm; and when to release his arm he gave the bear a violent kick, the brute let go his arm but seized his leg, which he bit in several places; but he soon became weak from loss of blood, and to Mr. Elliot's inexpressible relief and satisfaction he died, not before he had inflicted six severe wounds and several smaller ones. The animal, which I saw, weighed 480 pounds, and the peasants declared that last winter it devoured a woman and severely injured a man. Mr. Elliot had hardly time to think of the risk he ran, but said he felt very uncomfortable for a few seconds—first, before he was quite sure that the spear had run through the animal's body, for it was so sharp it hardly met any resistance; and then when the bear seized his hand, he expected to hear the bones crunched, but luckily the wounds were all flesh wounds, though one was close to the bone, and another very near the artery. The accident happened about 100 versts[1] from St. Petersburg, and Mr. Elliot returned home the same night in an open sledge with 15° of cold, Réaumur but so far from this having done harm, the doctor attributed his speedy recovery to this circumstance. Mr. Elliot told me he saw a great many wolf tracks, and in winter they even come within the barriers of the town. He mentioned one or two curious facts about these animals, viz., that if you come suddenly on a spot where wolves have been you will find that they are all huddled together, but on being approached they start off in different directions; but very soon the tracks lead to one point, and at last one track only s discernible. The wolf is a very sly animal, and a friend of ours, Mr. John Hamilton, who was a very keen sportsman, determined to try and catch one in a trap. He was astonished to find every morning that the bait had disappeared, but no wolf was caught; he found that the animal carefully trod in his own footsteps, and thus succeeded in carrying off the bait, so Mr. Hamilton, after setting his trap, lifted up the snow on which he had trodden, put his trap underneath it, and then replaced the snow. The next morning he found

[1] A verst is three quarters of a mile.

that this plan had succeeded, and the wolf was caught!

M. de Ribeaupierre came to see us, and related the following curious anecdote about a bear. Count Panin, who was M. de Ribeaupierre's intimate friend, was a great sportsman, and possessed a large property, about seventy versts from his château, where he went to shoot. Some years ago, in the month of September, M. de Ribeaupierre proposed paying Count Panin a visit at his château to celebrate his *fête* day. When the latter arrived, he found Count Panin was bear shooting, and for six successive days he had been following the tracks of two bears and their cubs without having an opportunity of getting near them. Count Panin received M. de Ribeaupierre's letter late in the afternoon, and being unwilling to return home without firing a shot, he still followed his game; and at last he heard a rustling in some bushes, and fancying it was a bear he fired, but as it was dark he would not venture into the thicket that evening, though he thought he heard moans. The next morning he returned to the spot; and there, sure enough, he found one of the cubs, which had been mortally wounded, but had dragged itself to a hollow tree, and there expired. Count Panin put it upon a telega, or open cart, and returned home full speed, arriving at his château just in time to welcome Count Ribeaupierre. The latter had retired to his room, and was dressing for dinner, when Count Panin rushed in and said his gamekeeper had just informed him that a large bear had been seen in the park, and as they were unknown in that part of the country, Count Panin proposed that immediately after dinner they should sally forth and shoot it. Accordingly they drove to the spot indicated by the keeper, and Count Panin shot a large she bear, which proved to be the poor cub's mother. She followed the track of the cart which bore her young one through seventy versts of open country, at the same speed as the post-horses. Such a curious instance of maternal love deserved to be commemorated, and Count Panin erected a monument to record this fact.

I have been told that my grandfather, Sir Harry Liddell, sent a hound by sea from Newcastle to London shortly after she had had puppies. The dog disappeared, and could not be found; but at the end of an incredibly short time she arrived at the kennel at Ravensworth a perfect skeleton, having run back 280 miles. The poor thing just got home, and then lay down and died!

CHAPTER VII.

Extract of Letter to the Hon. Mrs. Trotter—Return of the Emperor Nicholas from Palermo—The Church of Nôtre Dame de Casan—Laplanders on the Neva—Emperor's Choir—Count Nesselrode—Russian Carnivals—The Thaw—Visits to the Corps des Mines and the Hermitage—Presentation to the Emperor Nicholas.

St. Petersburg, January 27, 1846.—The thermometer was twenty-two degrees below zero when I got up this morning. I do not go out when it is as cold as this, but it was below zero when I walked yesterday, and I was so well wrapped up I came in quite hot. I am so pleased at having got some hyacinths and myrtles, which make my rooms look bright and pretty. Certainly one never appreciates the blessings and comforts one enjoys so abundantly in England till one knows what it is to be months without them. Half a dozen plants here give me as much, and perhaps more pleasure than a large conservatory full used to do. I watch every bud and every leaf, and feast my eyes upon the only bit of green I have seen since I came here.

The hyacinths are not outrageously expensive, but I asked the price of a common laurel we wished to buy, and that was between six and seven pounds sterling, so this will give you an idea of their value here. Little pots of holly and ivy were equally expensive, so when you look out at your beautiful beds of evergreens think of me!

St. Petersburg, March 30, 1846.—I am happy to say the weather has been milder lately; but there is a great deal of sickness here, and the typhus fever is carrying off more people than the cholera did in '32. One day last week it is said 850 people died of it, in a population of about 450,000. The upper classes are suffering very much from influenza; but one cannot wonder at sickness raging when one sees the sanitary condition of the place. The filth and dirt, which have been accumulating for the last five months, and which is thrown on the canals, is unthawing, and must poison the atmosphere. The varieties of bad smells in the streets are anything but agreeable, and I am rather glad that a bad cold in my head, which I have had for the last five weeks, has deadened my olfactory nerves. The ice is still nearly two feet thick in the streets, but it is as hard as a rock, and the men employed in clearing it away have difficulty in breaking it up with pickaxes. No one, to see the streets, could believe they are ice, for they look quite black; but you cannot conceive anything more atrocious than the state of the thoroughfares. They are full of immense holes, which threaten to upset the carriage every moment, and our good English springs get so terribly strained, that with five carriages of our own we have actually hired a Russian one for the time being.

St. Petersburg, May 21, 1847.—The plants you have kindly sent me arrived safely and in beautiful condition; but I am afraid I shall not be able to plant them out till the middle of June. You can have no conception how backward everything is here this spring. Except three fine days we have had nothing but the most bitter weather, with sleet and snow showers, and there are scarcely any vestiges of vegetation as yet. I drove to the Islands to-day in an open carriage, but was very glad of my large fur cloak and hot water bottle. Everything looks arid and sapless. I suppose whenever the weather does change the burst of spring will surprise us, but I think the spring here is far worse than the winter. One can make up one's mind to severe weather in December and January, but the end of May, when the days are so long (it is quite light till past 10 o'clock P.M.) and the sun is powerful, one does look for something more genial than frost and snow, particularly after having had them uninterruptedly for seven months!

Thank God! I am pretty well now, though so very thin my bones quite hurt me. I do long to get to the country, and hope we shall be settled there soon; but moving is a great business, for one has to take out all one's comforts, and every single article of furniture for the bedrooms. We feel so entirely cut off from the rest of the world, and especially from our own people, that the hope of seeing anyone from home is a great delight. Our last accounts from Ireland were a little less hopeless than they have been, and we trust the worst of the famine is nearly over, otherwise I really do not know what would happen; for our resources are well-nigh exhausted, and I cannot think what those landed proprietors who have nothing to depend upon but their rent will do. I had a very interesting letter from the Rev. Mr. Connolly the other day. He says the people themselves admit that the curse of blood cruelly spilt had fallen on the ground. At a relief committee he attended, some men said, 'Badly we deserve all this from your reverence, for faith we were often told that it would be no harm to kill you and all like you, because you asked us to read your "Book;" but now we know that you loved us, and we wish we could have that Book to learn to love God as you do, and each other as you have often told us we should.' God grant these feelings may be encouraged and strengthened, and our poor fellow-countrymen raised from the abyss of moral and physical degradation and misery in which they have been so long.

The Emperor Nicholas returned from Italy on January 11. He travelled, as he always did, with extraordinary rapidity, spent Christmas Day at Warsaw, and came on to St. Petersburg without stopping. He rested for three hours after his arrival, but attended the parade of the guards at eleven o'clock, after which he walked about the town and paid a number of visits. His activity was really remarkable. On the 13th H.I.M. received the gentlemen of the Corps Diplomatique; shook hands with my husband, and said, with reference to his marriage, which had taken place since last they had met, 'Ah! l'événement qui nous a causé tant d'inquiétude a donc eu lieu.'

During the Carnival masked balls take place frequently, and the Emperor always attended these, and often heard some very home truths. We were told that a gentleman of our acquaintance was rather making up to two ladies who were great friends, so they determined to *intriguer* him, and take it by turns to attend the masked balls, always telling each other what took place. As they were about the same height, dressed alike in a domino, and imitated each other's voices, the man was thoroughly taken in. On the last night of the Carnival he implored his partner to reveal her name, but this she positively refused to do, but promised him a rendezvous at Gatchina the following evening. Instead, however, of going there herself she sent her maid, and the gentleman, suspecting a hoax, sent his valet; therefore, these two, who were perfect strangers to each other, met, and the result was very ludicrous. The Russians consider it sinful to wear a mask, as they say that God made man's face, and he has therefore no right to conceal it; but, though wrong, they do it; and then, by way of washing away their sin, they jump into the Neva after the blessing of the waters on the Feast of the Epiphany, though the thermometer is then often many degrees below freezing.

The Bible is allowed in Russia, but it was published in Slavonic, which few people can read, and is very expensive. As late as the reign of the Emperor Alexander an ukase was printed forbidding a blessing to be carried in a hat. It seems that formerly when a Pope[1] was sent for to administer extreme unction, if anything hindered his going to the dying man he whispered a blessing in the messenger's hat, which was covered in his presence, and uncovered before the sick man, and this was supposed to convey a special blessing equivalent to the sacrament of extreme unction. When a baby was born, an icon, or image, with the head and hands painted, and the drapery in metal, was made the same size as the child, dedicated to the patron saint of the day of its birth, and hung up over the child's cradle. If the child died, the icon was often decorated with any jewellery which happened to have belonged to it, and sometimes they are richly decorated, and hung up as memorials in the churches.

Some years ago a priest translated the Psalms and New Testament into modern Russian, but as this work differed in some respects from the Authorised Version, the Emperor forbade its publi cation. We were told that an ambulating chapel had been sent to the Baltic provinces, and the

[1] In Russia the priests are called Popes.

Protestants were promised great privileges if they would join the Greek Church, which they did in great numbers; but it frequently happened that the men allowed themselves to be re-baptized, whilst the women and children remained Protestants. This caused great schism and distress in families, and after the peasants had joined the Greek Church the chapel moved on, and they were left without any religious instruction or means of worship, and found out too late that the promises on which they had relied were false; then, if they attempted to return to their own church, they were severely punished. Great distress prevailed in the Baltic provinces in the winter of 1845–6, and a number of poor people were starved to death. In the body of one man which was opened was found a quantity of leather, and in other cases the poor had mixed sawdust with their flour, which they could not digest. It often happened that the poor things left their homes and came to St. Petersburg in search of food. They walked several hundred versts, and the excitement kept them up during the journey, but they died in great numbers on arriving. One day a woman walked 300 versts with her daughter, reached one of the hospitals where she would have found relief, but sank from want and exhaustion an hour after her arrival. The Russians are generous, and one day when we had a large dinner party, I received a letter from my mother-in-law, mentioning the sad state of a clergyman's wife in Sussex, who had been left a widow with a large family totally unprovided for, her husband having suddenly died of apoplexy. I was much impressed by this story, and happened to mention it to Count Nesselrode, who was sitting next me at dinner. He immediately said, 'Why don't you make a collection for the widow?' I answered, 'I had not thought of doing so, as I imagined the Russians had poor enough of their own to support.' However, he said, 'If you will make a collection, I will give you a hundred roubles.' Encouraged by this offer, I mentioned the case to others, and had the satisfaction of sending home a cheque for one hundred pounds for the poor widow, to whom it came so unexpectedly that she quite felt it had been sent her by 'the Father of the fatherless, and the God of the widow.'

The gelinotte, a bird something between a grouse and a partridge, is common in Russia. Its plumage is grey, and it feeds principally upon the young shoots of the fir, which gives the flesh a strong flavour of turpentine, but otherwise it is good. The peasants have a tradition that the gelinotte was once the largest and finest bird in the forest; but it rebelled against the Great Spirit, and in consequence was reduced in size, while a portion of its flesh was given to the black-cock, who remained faithful in its allegiance, and it is thus that the Russian peasants account for the difference of colour in a black-cock's breast. The double snipes in August and September are excellent, and afford good sport to those who are fond of shooting. They are so fat at that season that it frequently happens they burst in falling, and they are really delicious. I am ashamed to say we also often had young black-cocks not larger than quails, which were also very good, and the ortalans from the south of Russia were supplied in great quantities. There is no salt-water fish at St. Petersburg, as the Baltic is fresh, and the ships take in their supply of water at Cronstadt; but the water of the Neva is unwholesome. The best fish are soudac, séguis, sturgeon, and sterlet; the latter is very delicate and good. There are fish boats on the Neva, and fish is taken all through the winter, by breaking the ice when the fish come up to breathe, and are easily caught. The caviare at St. Petersburg, which is considered a great luxury, is infinitely better than one can get elsewhere, as it is eaten fresh, whereas it must be salted before being exported. Sturgeon were Imperial property, and a high tax was put upon them. The Russians are very fond of a fish-soup, which is made of beer, fish, cucumbers, and various herbs. I thought it rather nasty, but the inhabitants relish it very much.

January 24, 1846.—The cold was very severe indeed—as much as 30 degrees of frost Réaumur, which is about 60 of Fahr. Breathing in such an atmosphere is painful, and makes one feel as if one were swallowing pins and needles. Long icicles hang from the horses' bits; the carriages make a crackling noise, as if they were passing over glass; and though the temperature indoors may be kept up to any heat, in the morning there was ice between the double windows, and I felt feverish and parched.

I heard a characteristic anecdote of the Emperor; viz. that when he was in Italy he found that the feld-jägers, or Government couriers, took longer time on their journeys than His Majesty considered necessary; and, on inquiry, it was proved that they were very much over-loaded with things for the different members of the Court, and carried all kinds of goods as well as despatches. To prevent the recurrence of this abuse, the Emperor now despatches the couriers himself, and the Ministers send their despatch-bags to him. There are terrible abuses in the Custom House; duty is so very high, everyone tries to evade it in every possible way. It is well known that a rich Russian noble, who had a service of plate sent from England, asked leave to have it examined at his own house. This was granted; but the officer who was sent to examine it received a large bribe, and consequently reported it at one quarter of its real value. When General Count Benkendorf was Minister of Police, on returning home one night from his club, he found his pocket-book, which was full of rouble notes, missing. He accordingly gave the police notice of the fact, stating the sum he had lost. A few days after this sum was returned to him, without the pocket-book, which was reported lost; but in the meantime it had been found, notes and all, in his fur pelisse, having slipped down between the lining and the cloth. The police, to show their zeal and activity, had collected the money among themselves, and presented it to their superior officer!

February 5, 1846.—We visited the Cathedral of Nôtre Dame de Casan, the first stone of which was laid by the Emperor Alexander in 1801. It is built in the form of a cross, and the interior is very magnificent, divided by a double row of granite Corinthian columns, with bronze bases and chapiters. The keys of the different fortresses taken by the Russians are kept there; and there is also a large collection of standards—among others I noticed some of the French Imperial eagles. Afternoon service commenced whilst we were in the Cathedral, which was attended by about fifty or sixty people of all classes, who approached the altar, where they remained alternately standing and crossing themselves, kneeling and touching the ground with their foreheads, whilst the priests chanted the service in a monotonous tone of voice. These priests were dressed in a simple black caftan; but presently another priest, attired in a magnificent cloth of gold cope, and carrying a silver censer, appeared, and walked about incensing the various pictures of saints. Afterwards a number of candles were lighted, the two large doors at the back of the altar were flung open, and showed a picture of the Assumption of the Virgin. During the whole time the priests continued chanting, but occasionally the one in the cope said something to which the others seemed to respond. At the end of a few minutes the doors were closed, and the service went on as before. There was no music, but the priests had fine voices.

The Czar always went to the Casan Church before commencing or returning from a journey, and also when any great event occurred. He went without form or ceremony, knelt before the altar, and prostrated himself. There seemed no particular form of worship, the congregation either knelt or stood as they pleased; but no one is allowed to sit in the Greek Church. There were a number of small altars before the various pictures, and high up over the high altar there was a large representation of the Last Supper. No woman is permitted within the rails of the altar; and should such a thing occur accidentally, the church is considered desecrated, and must be re-consecrated. Both sexes partake of the Holy Communion, which is also administered to infants. The consecrated elements are on no account to be allowed to fall, so when an infant offers opposition to taking them, its mouth is held open and the priest puts them down its throat. During parts of the service the words 'Gospodi, Gospodi Pamilui'—'Lord, have mercy on us,'—are repeated very frequently and rapidly by the deacons, sometimes forty times running, and the voices seem to rise in a sort of gamut.

February 9.—We went to see some Laplanders, who had established themselves with their reindeer on the Neva. They lived in a small hut made of hides, within which was a woman and child dressed entirely in fur, lying on a couch of the same. The men were excessively ugly, with very dark complexions, flat noses, and eyes which turned up at the corners. They are entirely clothed in fur, and wear a small skull-cap of the same. They drive in wooden sledges drawn by four reindeer, and fly along at tremendous speed, looking very wild. We also visited one of the fish boats, and saw a quantity of various kinds of frozen fish, immense sturgeon and sterlet from the Volga, perch, pike, smelts, cod, and a large flat fish. The large fish are sawn in half, and it was very curious to see them frozen as hard as stone. The caviare is kept in barrels, and the man offered us two little wooden sticks, like the Chinese chop-sticks, to partake of some, which I declined. The vegetables in Russia are generally preserved, but it is difficult to tell them from fresh.

February 21.—I went to a private rehearsal of the choir of the Emperor's chapel, and I was surprised and delighted with the beauty of the music, which certainly exceeded any I had ever heard. I only regretted that the music was performed in too small a room for the voices to be sufficiently appreciated; the effect would have been so much grander had I been at a greater distance from the choir. There were about eighty-six voices altogether, which was not the full complement; but with his usual magnificence, the Emperor sent twelve of the finest voices to Rome, that on her arrival there the Empress might have her own choir. Nothing could exceed the beauty of the voices, and their gradual swelling and decreasing was very striking. On another occasion, General Lwoff, who was himself a great musician, was ordered by the Emperor to superintend the practising of the various choirs of the regiments of Guards quartered at St. Petersburg. This he did for a year and a half, and then invited me to come and hear them. There were six hundred and thirty voices, without accompaniment. The finest voices come from White Russia; but whenever any one throughout the Empire has an unusually rich voice he is engaged, and certainly I never heard such voices—from the deepest diapason bass to the highest tenor. Bartniansky's music is very impressive. The words are Slavonic; and those which are sung during the administration of the

Holy Communion are in the following sense: 'Let us not approach Thee, O Lord, in this Thy holy sacrament, like the traitor Judas, who betrayed Thee with a kiss; but as the thief upon the cross, let us, with deep humility and unfeigned sorrow, confess our own sinfulness, and cry, "Lord, remember me."'

The Emperor was very proud of his choir. The boys were dressed in a simple uniform, and we saw the preparations for their dinner. General Lwoff composed the Russian National Hymn, 'Boje Tsar Chrani;' and he told me that once he was travelling on the Rhine, when a brass band came and performed it very badly under his windows. His *amour propre* as the composer was so injured, that he sent for the leader of the band and told him that if he would bring him the score he would correct it, as it was all wrong. The man accordingly brought him the music, which he took pains to rectify, and then he made the men repeat it several times till they played it correctly, when he told them they might go; but the leader said he would not do so until he was paid one hundred francs. That General Lwoff had kept them for two hours for his own gratification—though it was a matter of perfect indifference to them whether they played his composition right or wrong—and therefore he was bound to pay them the loss of their time.

I had a visit from Count Nesselrode, who but lately arrived from Italy. He was not a striking man, as he was very short, looked rather Jewish, and wore spectacles ; but his conversation was very clever and animated, and his manner perfectly easy. He was delighted with his first visit to Italy, and also spoke with much pleasure of the visit he paid to England two years ago. He is a most remarkable man, having been at the head of affairs in Russia for the last twenty-seven years, and before that he bore a distinguished part at the Congress of Vienna. He is particularly shrewd and clever, an excellent man of business, and altogether well fitted for the important post he filled. Count Nesselrode was christened on board an English frigate in the Tagus, and always considered himself a member of the Church of England. In Russia no official can receive his salary till he can prove that he has received the Holy Communion in whatever church he belongs to. Consequently, once a year, generally on Holy Thursday, Count Nesselrode, when Chancellor of the Empire and Minister for Foreign Affairs, used to attend the English Chapel on the English

Quay, and receive the Holy Communion according to the forms of the Church of England, which, however, he never attended on other occasions, or, I believe, any other place of worship, though of course he had to be officially present at all the great ceremonies of the Greek Church. I remember his dining with us in January, 1848, and his saying to me that no political event seemed of any importance nowadays. '*Quand tout sa comme un papier de musique!*'

Within a very few weeks after that the whole of Europe was in a blaze—revolution broke out in Prussia, Austria, and France. Louis Philippe was driven out of Paris, the Tuileries were sacked, and the Republic was declared. Well might one exclaim, Who can tell what a day may bring forth?

The intelligence of the projected marriage of the Grand Duchess Olga to the Crown Prince of Wurtemberg caused great pleasure to the Emperor.

The Prince met the Emperor at Vienna, and there he told him that though he (the Emperor) did not wish to influence his or the Grand Duchess's inclinations in any way, nothing would afford him greater satisfaction than seeing them united; and therefore he freely consented to the

Crown Prince's intention of going to Palermo with a view of trying to engage the Grand Duchess's affections. The Prince accordingly went to Palermo where he met with a gracious reception from the Empress and her daughter, and at the end of five days he proposed and was accepted, to the great satisfaction of all parties.

The Carnival opened on Tuesday, February 22, 1846. The day was bright and fine—the first time it had been enjoyable for many weeks. The whole of the great Place de l'Amirauté was filled with temporary booths and wooden theatres, circus, roundabouts, ice hills, &c. &c., for the amusement of the lower orders. The road opposite the Winter Palace was lined with carriages, which paraded in regular succession, most of them filled with children. Altogether the sight was gay and pretty, like a large fair. During the Carnival week people of all classes seemed quite demented, their one thought being how much amusement and dissipation they could crowd into it. The theatres were open morning and evening. Private parties began in the afternoon, and dancing was kept up till a late hour.

The last party was given by H.I.H. the Grand Duchess Marie of Leuchtenberg, 'pour enterrer le Carnaval,' as the Russians said. Dancing commenced at three o'clock P.M. At six the company retired to dine and change their dress—they returned at eight; and though dancing should have ceased as the clock struck twelve, the guests did not retire till a late hour. During Lent the theatres are closed, no balls are given, and the fast was so strictly observed that the common people ate no meat whatever; and even the upper classes would not touch sugar which had been refined with blood, and put lemon instead of milk into their tea. Great sickness was caused by the sudden transition from feasting to fasting; and the food, which was very unwholesome, consisted principally of dried and often bad fish, decayed cabbage, dried fungus or gribuis, which the Russians are very fond of. The consequence was, that there was a greater prevalence of fever during Lent than at any other season of the year; but this may also have been owing to the break-up of the frost, because during the winter all the drainage and offal of the town was thrown upon the canals. When these unfroze the stench was dreadful; the streets during the thaw were in the most terrible state, as the ice, which was often several feet thick, was broken up and left to melt, so it was almost impossible to drive either in a sledge or a carriage; and the roads were full of deep holes, which threatened to break not only every spring in our carriage, but every bone in our skin!

March 10.—We went to see Count Nesselrode's villa at Kamini Ostroff, and the Botanical Gardens. The flowers at the villa were in great beauty; the camellias, especially, were as fine as any I ever saw in England, and the greenhouses were beautifully arranged and very extensive. The houses in the Botanical Gardens were also very large, and we walked a mile before we had gone through them. The Gardens were created by Peter the Great; but after his death they were much neglected till 1822, when they were put into good order, and Mr. Fisher was appointed manager. He had the care of them for many years; but was only allowed 2000*l.* a year for keeping them up, and had only twenty men under him. As there were above two hundred thousand plants in the collection, and these required constant attention, &c. &c., he complained that he had not hands enough to do the work properly. Some of the tropical plants were very fine, and a house was being erected for them two hundred and sixty feet long and sixty-seven high. There were not many flowers in bloom, and the collection is more scientific than ornamental; but I particularly admired the *Maranta sanguinea* and the *Narcissus angustifolia*, the *Primula nevalis*, and the *Acacia hertulata*. There was also a small bright purple azalea, called *Rodosa*, which was very pretty.

March 20, 1846.—We visited the Corps des Mines with Count Rayneval, our French colleague, who was a very clever, agreeable man. We looked over a very large collection of minerals, antediluvian remains, models, &c. &c., and were much struck by one fine nugget of gold which weighed eighty pounds. There was a large collection of uncut precious stones—emeralds, rubies, sapphires, beryls, and garnets—still embedded in the rock in which they were found. We descended to a subterranean passage, which is arranged exactly like the various mines in Russia, and the strata are accurately preserved. The head of the establishment afterwards pointed out to me some of the most interesting models, among others the one which showed how the gold dust is separated from the sand in Siberia. The sand is placed in a long trough, underneath which there is a reservoir of water; this is admitted through cocks into different trays. Men are constantly employed in raking the sand, which is carried away by the water; but the gold dust sinks, and is carefully preserved.

April 10, 1846.—The ice on the Neva, which for some time had looked very black and porous, began to move. The stream first appeared in the middle of the river, and the next morning the ice was gone! None but those who have experienced it, can know the delightful sensation of feeling that the winter is indeed over. The impracticability of moving during the winter months (there were then no railways in Russia) made me feel exactly as if I were in prison, and when the ice disappeared I felt as if the prison doors had been thrown open, and home became accessible. The river presented a most curious appearance. Huge masses of ice were floating down, some railed round looking like skating grounds; others, covered with heaps of snow, like small pyramids; and while at one moment the river was almost clear, at another it was blocked with pieces of ice of every variety of shape and size. When the ice breaks up, the Governor of the Fortress goes, according to an ancient custom, to the Czar, and presents a goblet of fresh water to his Imperial Majesty, who returns it filled with gold ducats. Then he rows down the river in his State barge to show that the navigation is safe, and shortly afterwards the ferry boats are seen plying in all directions; but they are never allowed till the Governor has crossed over the Neva from the Fortress. The ice lasts on an average one hundred and forty-six days, but this year, 1846, it only lasted one hundred and twenty. The season had been unhealthy. Typhus fever raged among the lower classes, and carried off more people than the cholera did; and instead of forty-six deaths, which is the average a day, as many as one hundred and forty died within twenty-four hours. The hospitals were so crowded the poor could not gain admittance; and I was told by Dr. Rogers that no less than fifty cases were refused in one day, most of whom were in the last stage of disease—actually dying. The fever was first brought into the town from the provinces, where there had been a great scarcity of provisions. It was so catching, that all the attendants at the hospitals suffered from it more or less, especially the laundresses; but it was almost entirely confined to the lower classes. The upper classes suffered severely from influenza, which was so prevalent that very few persons escaped.

Easter Eve, April 18, 1846.—The weather has been bright during the last week, but bitterly cold, with sharp north-easterly winds. The ice began coming down from the Ladoga Lake; the Place de l'Amirauté was again filled precisely as it was during the last week of the Carnival, for the celebration of Easter. I was unfortunately prevented by indisposition from attending the midnight mass in the chapel at the Winter Palace. The Court all attend in full dress, the music is very fine, and the Czar embraces those present, saying, 'Christus vos Krest!' (Christ is risen), which is the Russian salutation on Easter Day. I was told that once the Emperor greeted the sentinel with those words who, to his astonishment, responded 'that is a lie.' On inquiry it turned out that the man was a Jew.

We went to the Woronzow Daschkow's to see a French play acted by amateurs, called 'Le Mari à la Campagne,' and 'La Fille à marier.' The players were Countesses Woronzow, Bray, Madame Salavoy, and Madame Orloff Denisoff, Monsieur de Jomini, Count Bylandt, and M. Albedinsky, who would all have done credit to any stage.

I visited the Winter Palace and the far-famed Hermitage, and was delighted and astonished at their splendour and size; but I was struck there, as elsewhere in this curious town, with the roughness and want of finish one sees at every turn. Splendid palaces over shops, shabby liveries, carriages and four with ragged postillions, noble stone staircases with dirty green baize carpeting, and a general appearance of dirt and untidiness which is distressing to an eye accustomed to English neatness and cleanliness.

We saw the collection of pictures left by M. Tatischeff, late Russian Ambassador at Vienna, to the Emperor, but they are most of them allowed to be copies, and not very good. We then proceeded to the Gallery lately constructed to contain the pictures of the Romanoff dynasty, from the first Patriarch who ascended the throne, to the present Emperor and his children; but their portraits were not completed. I was delighted with the *chef-d'œuvres* at the Hermitage, especially the Dutch school, which is the finest in the world, and rich in Rembrandts, Wouvermans, P. Potters, Teniers, Berghems, Van Osts, and Ruysdaals. The Italian school is much poorer, far from complete, and I doubt the veracity of some of the pictures said to be originals. Besides the pictures, there is a large collection of curiosities; among the rest some very ancient ornaments, gold chaplets, &c. &c., which were discovered in tombs in the Crimea. Some of the bracelets resembled in shape and make the Indian ornaments, and there was also a fine collection of gems, caskets, goblets, &c. &c. We saw lastly the theatre belonging to the Palace, where the Empress Katherine had private theatricals. It is now dismantled, and the Loges de Raphael are packed up in wooden cases. We saw a curious piece of German mechanism made during the reign of the Empress Katherine—an owl, a peacock, and a cock on a golden tree. The owl moves its head and eyes, and beats time with its claw to music played by bells. The peacock moves its head and feathers, turns round and spreads its tail with all the pride and dignity of the real bird. The cock also moves its head and crows loudly. This curiosity was taken to England, and at one time there was a question of its being bought and sent to India; but the price demanded was too exorbitant, so it was brought to St. Petersburg and sold to Prince Potemkin. After his death it came to the Empress Katherine.

Over the riding house of the Palace there is a garden, and it is curious to walk up eighty or one hundred steps, and then suddenly find a large garden planted with trees and shrubs, broad gravel walks, flower beds, &c. &c. At one time the trees had grown to a considerable size, but some time since repairs were required, and they have not grown large again, though the lilacs were a good size. The Russians have very magnificent ideas about their winter gardens. One day I was complaining to the Grand Duchess Marie, that I missed the evergreens I was used to at home, so she said, 'Mais, Madame, vous avez donc une cour, pourquoi ne pas créer un jardin d'hiver!' As if it was the simplest thing in the world to glaze the court of a hired house and turn it into a garden! Truly, I thought, 'l'impossible est seulement dans le dictionnaire des fous!' as Napoleon said.

Friday, May 8.—I met the Emperor Nicholas for the first time at a party given by the Woronzow Daschkoffs. I arrived late, in consequence of the milliner not sending my dress till the last moment, and the play had already begun. However, I was pushed on to the front row, and had no sooner taken my seat, when the Emperor observed me, and I saw him evidently asking the Hereditary Grand Duke who I was, after which he looked at me for some time. As soon as the act was over, the Grand Duchess Marie came up and shook hands with me, expressing her pleasure at seeing me again. Then the Emperor came up, and talked to me for a long time. He was certainly the finest, handsomest man I ever saw, and his voice and manner were most attractive. He expressed regret at not having made my acquaintance sooner, hoped I had not suffered from the severity of the climate, adding that he did not remember such intense cold and such damp as we had had for some months. I ventured to insinuate that as His Imperial Majesty had come straight from Palermo in the month of December, he probably felt the sudden change very much; and this he allowed had been the case. His Majesty asked much after the Queen, and said how greatly he wished she could be induced to visit St. Petersburg, though he feared the distance was almost too great for him to expect that pleasure. When first the Emperor approached me I felt very shy, but such was his kindness and gentleness of manner, that before he left me I felt quite at my ease. The difference in his countenance when speaking to ladies, and when he is commanding his troops, is very remarkable. He looked thinner than he did when I saw him in England in 1844, and he was dressed in a plain uniform, and moved without the least ceremony. Instead of sitting opposite the stage in the first row, the Emperor chose a small chair on one side close to the musicians; and though he frequently smiled and applauded, the expression of his fine countenance was grave, almost sad. After the performance, the Grand Duke Michael requested my husband to present him to me, when he talked to me for some time, referred with pleasure to his visit to England, and said how much gratified he had been by a kind letter of condolence he had received from the Queen, when he lost his daughter a year and a half ago.

May 11, 1844.—We went to a fine ball at Count Colloredo's, the Austrian Ambassador, which was attended by the Czar and Imperial family. Out of compliment, gentlemen were requested to wear full uniform. The Emperor and Grand Dukes wore Austrian uniforms, which were more becoming and much handsomer than the simple General's uniform they usually wear, and the Emperor looked, if possible, handsomer than ever. He again came up and talked to me, and told me of the arrival of the first English steamer that year, which is always rather an event at St. Petersburg. He seemed almost annoyed that there were only six passengers on board, and asked me if I did not expect some of my relations or friends; and when I answered 'No,' His Majesty shook his head, and said he feared I had not reported favourably of his capital and the Russian climate, adding that he should have much pleasure in seeing any of my family or friends! I conversed with the Grand Dukes Héritier and Michael, and with the Duc de Leuchtenberg, who amused me by complaining that the Emperor and 'leurs altesses' filled up all the doors; and that therefore, 'il n'y avait pas moyen de circuler,' he himself being almost in the door-way at that moment. The ball-room was most brilliantly lighted, and the house, the Palais Soltykoff on the great quay, is exceedingly fine; the quantity of servants in State liveries, who lined the staircase, made the first entry very striking. Count Colloredo not being then married, Baroness Seebach, the wife of the Saxon Minister, *née* Nesselrode, did the honours. Supper was served upon small round tables for twelve, but there was no profusion of plate.

May 13.—This being the Russian May-day, there was a *fête* at Katerinhof, which is the Longchamps of St. Petersburg. Though the wind was cold, the weather was bright and fine, and an immense crowd turned out on foot and in every kind of conveyance, so that the whole road to Katerinhof was lined with carriages and foot-passengers, and the scene was very animated, pretty, and characteristic. There was the chinovnik (merchant), evidently well to do in the world, seated in a droschky, side by side with his wife, who, turned out in her holiday costume, generally appeared much younger than her mate. The various uniforms were very striking, especially the Cossack and Circassian, and the contrast of the features of the several nations most remarkable. Vegetation was very backward—the trees scarcely budding.

CHAPTER VIII.

Parade on the Champs de Mars—The Empress Katherine, her Death—The Isaac Church—Visit to Tzarskoe Selo and Peterhof—Visit to Hanover—Return to England—Marriage of the Grand Duchess Olga—Death of my father-in-law, Benjamin, Lord Bloomfield—We visit the Rhine—Curious ghost story—Berlin—Return to Russia—Blessing of the Neva—I am presented to the Empress—Funeral of Prince Vassiltchikoff—Christening in the Winter Palace—Easter Eve.

May 14, 1846.—I witnessed a magnificent sight—the Emperor Nicholas reviewing forty thousand men on the Champs de Mars. The day was fine and bright, and I had an excellent place at a window in the Duke of Oldenburgh's palace. At one o'clock—the troops being then all on the ground—the Emperor and his suite, which also comprised all the military men in the Corps Diplomatique—my husband among the rest—rode up and down the ranks, the troops cheering, and the sound of such a multitude of voices was quite thrilling. The Emperor then took his stand near the summer garden, and all the troops defiled before him. First, the Infantry, then the Light Artillery, then the

Cavalry, followed by the Heavy Artillery. As the weather was still cold the Infantry wore their winter clothing, and though they marched well, their appearance was not nearly so striking as the Cavalry regiments. These were headed by a small body of Circassians, in their scarlet uniforms, covered with coat of mail, and they charged without much regard to order, and looked very wild. The regular motion of the bayonets of the Infantry resembled the waving of a field of corn in the summer breeze, the glitter of the helmets and the brilliant colours of the cavalry were quite dazzling. The Emperor Nicholas looked superb, the Grand Dukes Héritier and Michael rode at his side, and the air was positively rent with the cheers of the mighty mass of human beings who, all dependent upon the Sovereign's will, anxiously awaited the approving look which told them that he was satisfied. When he testifies approval, the soldiers answer, 'We rejoice, father; but we will try and do better next time.' I little thought when looking at those troops that in a few short years many of them would be fighting the English and French in the Crimea, from which the large majority never returned. We heard that regiments which left the North one thousand strong, had dwindled to two hundred men before a shot was fired; and after the war was over Sir Fenwick Williams, who traversed the length of the land when Kars capitulated, told me he could scarcely see an able-bodied man cultivating the soil—nothing remained in the villages, but old men and females.

At a dinner we gave on the 19th, Count Bloudoff, who was a great talker and very agreeable, told me some interesting anecdotes about Dr. Rogerson, who was the Empress Katherine's physician. Perhaps had she listened to his advice her life might have been prolonged; for the day before she was seized with the apoplectic fit which killed her, Dr. Rogerson dined at the Hermitage. That morning the Empress had received the intelligence of an important victory, the news of which elated her very much; and during the evening she looked so flushed and excited that Dr. Rogerson was struck by her manner, and when she took leave of her guests he followed her to her room, and begged to be allowed to feel her pulse. That caused him so much anxiety, he ordered her to be bled instantly. The Empress, however, laughed at his fears, declined his advice, saying it would be time enough on the morrow; but at four o'clock in the morning she was struck by the hand of death, and never rallied.

Dr. Rogerson, who was fond of society, and liked a game at whist, was furious with a certain Princess G——, who was in the habit of sending for him at most inconvenient seasons to prescribe for imaginary ailments. She sent for him once in the middle of the night, saying that she was dying, and begged him to come instantly. When he arrived he found that, as usual, it was a false alarm; however, he looked very serious, assured the Princess she was in great danger, and that he was not at all sure he could save her; but she must instantly drink several glasses of cold water, and get up and walk fifty times up and down the English Quay. As the night was bitterly cold, and it was snowing hard, this was considered an extraordinary remedy for a dying woman; but, however, the learned physician insisted, and took his leave. The Princess, in fear and trembling, got out of her bed, and placing implicit trust in the efficacy of the remedy, followed the Doctor's advice. The following day Dr. Rogerson called, and found his patient perfectly well; he then told her that he had been so perpetually annoyed by being called in without necessity, he had determined upon giving her a lesson, and he hoped henceforward his services would be dispensed with, except in case of real necessity.

Saturday, May 30, 1846.—The weather was beautiful, and the evening so mild, we drove from nine to eleven in the open carriage, and the air was delicious. There is no night at this season of the year, the sun scarcely disappears for more than two or three hours, the sky is always light, and the atmosphere often hot; but the frost hardly gets thoroughly out of the ground—July being the only month in the year one is safe from frost. People began to move out to the Islands, boats and carts full of furniture were constantly going forth, and the move is one of the important events of the year. We had the double windows taken out, which is always pleasant, as the want of fresh air in the house is very trying. One side of our house looking to the river was hermetically sealed in winter, and though I had a 'Was ist das,' or single pane, made to open in my bedroom and boudoir, this caused such a draught in the cold weather, that I was sometimes obliged to leave the room.

June 1st.—We visited the Isaac's Church with Mr. Baird. The interior was unfinished, except a very small portion, where there are still the remains of the old church. In Russia a church may not be entirely demolished and rebuilt, but a portion of the old structure must always be retained. I admired the model of the old church almost more than the new. We went into Vitali's *ateliers*, and saw some of his models—a large bas-relief of the Adoration of the Magi over the north door is very fine. The paintings in the interior are all by Neff, Bruloff, Bruno; and Montferrand is the architect. The dome is built on a new principle, and is entirely formed of cast iron. We ascended two hundred and seventy-five steps to the cupola on the top of the church, and the view from thence is very extensive; but the country all round St. Petersburg is so perfectly flat that it is uninteresting, and the town itself, with its many gilt domes and spires, is what strikes the eye most. We were told that Montferrand had made a picture representing an inundation at St. Petersburg, and the only two objects which were visible were the Isaac's Church and the Alexander pillar, which were both constructed by him!—rather characteristic of French vanity.

This reminds me of an anecdote of my dear husband, who was taken to Paris when he was fifteen by his father, and one day ascended the pillar in the Place Vendôme. There he found an old soldier of the guard, who showed him Paris, and then said, 'N'est-ce pas, Monsieur, Paris est bien plus grand, et bien plus beau que Londres.' This excited the young Englishman's anger, and he answered, 'Quant à cela, on ôterait tout Paris de Londres sans s'en apercevoir!'

We visited the manufactory where the eight malachite pillars ordered by the Emperor are being constructed. The pillars are first cast in bronze, then the malachite, about half-an-inch thick, is laid upon it in innumerable small pieces, cemented together with a composition made of malachite and mastic, and then the whole is polished.

June 2, 1846.—We went to see the private apartments in the Winter Palace and the Crown Jewels, which are kept in glass cases. Some of the diamonds were very large and fine. The Emperor and Empress' crowns are entirely composed of diamonds set clear, and at the top of the Emperor's crown there is a famous ruby of immense size. The diamond which forms the top of the sceptre is also enormous, and there were several splendid necklaces, earrings, and *parures* of emeralds and diamonds, rubies and diamonds, pearls and diamonds, sapphires—in short, nearly all the fine jewels except those the Empress took to Italy. We saw the Empress' *salon*, a very pretty room, looking on the Neva, from which one passes into a covered garden filled with exotics. We also saw the Emperor's small private chapel, where divine service is performed daily, and the apartments of the Czarewna, and the late Grand Duchess Alexandrine, which last were fitted up at the time of her marriage to the Prince of Hesse, and have never been used since her death. Almost all the Malmaison collection of pictures, which were removed from the Hermitage, have been hung up in some large apartments beyond those of the Czarewna, and I was much delighted with them, especially with a wonderful Paul Potter, representing a farm with various groups of horses and other animals, and some beautiful Murillos, Claudes, Rubens, and Poussins—all of which are to be taken to the Hermitage when the gallery which is in process of construction is completed.

June 9, 1846.—M. Sabouroff having kindly offered to take us to see Tzarskoe Selo and Pavloffsky, we went there by the one o'clock train. We found a pony carriage waiting, and drove first to the new palace built by the Emperor Alexander. The Emperor and Empress' private apartments have been completely altered since the death of their lovely daughter, the Grand

Duchess Alexandrine, in order that no trace of that painful event should recall it to the Empress' mind. The room where the Grand Duchess died has been divided into three, but the place where her bed stood is completely separated and turned into an oratory. Some very fine old Dresden china now in the Empress' boudoir was discovered in an attic where it had been cast aside as lumber. The Emperor's apartment is small, and contains models of all the different cavalry regiments in Russia, beautifully executed; there were also a number of modern pictures representing different battles and parades. I remarked a great many fought by the Emperor Napoleon, for whom the Czar had a great admiration.

After seeing the Palace, we drove to the Farm, which was only remarkable for its extreme neatness and cleanliness—a rare thing in Russia. We then went to see a very fine elephant, which has been sent from Persia, thirteen feet high, and large in proportion. It seems that during the great inundation of 1826 the waters entered an elephant's stable. The keeper, in order to escape, got up into the manger; but as the water rose the elephant thought the man was playing him a trick, so he kept sucking the water up in his trunk and shooting it at his keeper, who was nearly drowned.

We drove to a pretty spot where a summer-house has been erected to the memory of the Grand Duchess Alexandrine, as it was a favourite spot of hers when she went to feed her swans. The Emperor has erected a monument in black and white marble, where a statue of the Grand Duchess is placed in a niche, holding a baby in her arms, and she is represented as in the act of ascending to heaven. The head is said to be like, but the body is too long and out of proportion. The drive through the park to the arsenal was very pretty, and the whole place was beautifully kept. The day was bright and fine, so we saw it to advantage; and as the trees were clad in the first brilliant green of spring, vegetation looked more luxuriant than any I had yet seen in Russia; but the growth is almost entirely confined to birch, fir, oak, elm, and lime. The three latter are rather rare, and there is but little variety in the drive through long straight alleys, but they are very extensive, and there are as many as one hundred and thirty versts of drive in the park. The arsenal is a Gothic tower, where there is a large and fine collection of armour and different kinds of arms, also two splendid Turkish saddle-cloths and accoutrements, embroidered in diamonds; a breakfast service which belonged to Napoleon, and a lock of his hair sent from St. Helena after his death. From the Arsenal we drove to the Gardens. As nothing flourishes in Russia out of doors through the winter, all the fruit trees are under glass, and consequently the range of greenhouses is immense. Then we drove to 'La Chine,' where there is a collection of small houses which are inhabited by the attendants of the Court during a residence at Tzarskoe Selo, and then we went to see the Chapel and apartments at the Old Palace, where the Grand Duke Héritier was living. The chapel is very richly decorated in blue and gold, and the ante-room leading to it is white and gold.

The Emperor Alexander's apartments are just as they were when he left them. His writing materials, scissors, pens, &c. &c., lying on his table; and his coat, boots, hat, gloves, and shirt laid out in his bed-room. The bed was very small, and looked particularly uncomfortable, as did also his shaving apparatus—there never was a room with less air of luxury than his. From Tzarskoe we drove through the park to Pavloffsky, where the Grand Duke Michael has a palace. The ground is prettily varied, and the Vauxhall, where we dined, is a favourite resort in the summer. Every *fête* day crowds go down by the railroad from St. Petersburg, and a number of people live in villas there during the summer months. As the Imperial grounds are open to the public, it is one of the nicest places near St. Petersburg.

June 12, 1846.—We started immediately after breakfast in an open carriage, and drove to Peterhof. The weather was very fine, with a hot sun and pleasant breeze. There are villas and gardens on each side of the road, with occasional glimpses of the gulf, and though it is not particularly striking, the fresh green of spring made it look bright and pretty. As we had not been able to make arrangements beforehand we depended entirely on ourselves and our jäger, and when first we arrived at the Great Palace at Peterhof, things seemed rather hopeless, for we could only find some workpeople about, and could not make ourselves understood. At last, however, we found one of the Court servants, who spoke German, and he showed us all over the palace. It was being prepared for the Grand Duchess Olga's marriage. The architecture reminded me of an old French palace; the church had just been re-gilt, as the marriage was to be solemnised there. The preparations for the illuminations were erected. A framework, twenty or thirty feet high, lined each alley, which was to be entirely covered with coloured lamps; and as the alleys are numerous, the effect must resemble Alladdin's wonderful garden in the 'Arabian Nights.' On the *fête* day the grounds are thrown open to the public, and everyone who can goes to Peterhof. The guests are to be invited to a ball, and will drive up and down the illuminated alleys in *chars-à-bancs.*

From the great palace we drove to the Empress' cottage. The rooms there are quite small, simply furnished, and the view from the windows, which were plate glass, was beautiful. The Empress was expected, and a number of pictures commemorating her visit to Palermo had been hung up. All her things were lying about her boudoir; and on one side of the house there was a beautiful statue of the Virgin by Vitali. It is enclosed on three sides with trees and flowers, and faces a fine view of the grounds and gulf. Another small cottage close by was inhabited by the young Grand Dukes, Michael and Nicholas, and we saw the place where they practised their gymnastic exercises. The place was full of flowers, and must be very enjoyable. From the cottage we drove along the shores of the gulf to Mon Bijou, which is a large pavilion with a terrace over the gulf, and some good-sized trees. When the actors and actresses are summoned to Peterhof they are lodged there. We next proceeded to Marly, a small palace that was inhabited by Peter the Great. His coats, hats, boots, sticks, and bed are still preserved there, and it is said that one of the rooms was wainscotted by his own hands. There is a fishpond in front of the palace full of old carp, which come to be fed when a bell is rung. These are of enormous size, and have a small chain round their necks, which was put on during the life of Peter the Great. From Marly we passed on to the English Palace, which is inhabited by the Corps Diplomatique during the *fêtes*, and then visited the pheasantry, farm, and after a long drive arrived at the Isba, or Russian cabin, which is a lovely little log-house, where the Empress occasionally went to have tea.

Then we saw the Isola Madre and the Isola Bella, two islands on an artificial lake, where Italian buildings were being erected for the Empress: these would make very good houses, and are surrounded with gardens, flowers, and statues. People in general are not allowed to visit these islands, but as we were bent on seeing everything, we bribed a gardener to ferry us across in a miserable little cranky raft which was used for carrying flower-pots, so it was full of mud and dirt. A soldier brought us back, but as he did not understand the management of our

P 2

frail barque he kept turning round and round, and I fully expected that we should be upset in the middle of the lake; but by good luck more than good management we landed safely, and after resting at a little public-house, called the Samson, where we lunched, we drove six versts further to the Grand Duchess Marie's palace at Serguieffsky. The situation of the house was pretty, and more elevated than is usual in this flat country. As the Grand Duchess was out we did not drive up, but returned to Peterhof, and went to a place called Znamenska, where the Grand Duchess Olga was to spend her honeymoon. One room was very characteristic of Russia, for the columns were covered with trellis work and ivy, and formed a vaulted roof, above which the ceiling rose. The effect was pretty and singular. We stopped to see Strelna on our way home, a large palace which was inhabited by the late Grand Duke Constantine, but has not been inhabited since his death. On Saturday, June 13, we left St. Petersburg, having been summoned to England by the serious illness of my dear father-in-law. After a rough and disagreeable passage we landed at Lubeck, and never can I forget the delightful change in the feeling of the air, and the sight of the lovely flowers which we bought for a penny! When we left Russia the lilacs were only just budding, the tulips, narcissus, and other spring flowers were out; but the drive from Lubeck to Hamburg in the cool of the evening was delightful—the air perfumed with honeysuckle and wild flowers. I was struck by the immense quantity of cranes, which were all building, and we saw a nest upon almost every farmhouse along the road.

At Lubeck, M. Benecke, the Consul, brought me a box, which he said had arrived for me by the last messenger from England; as he did not know what it contained, I did not even open it till we got to Hamburg. Then I found it was neither more nor less than two jewel cases—one of turquoises and diamonds, the other sapphires and diamonds. My husband, much surprised, asked me whether I expected any jewels from England, and on my answering in the negative he said they must have been sent by some jeweller to my address to escape duty, and that it was a great liberty. So we carefully repacked them, and brought them back to England. My brother-in-law, Colonel Kingscote, met us on our arrival, and his first words were, 'Have you received the jewels?' We said 'Yes; but what are they?' He then told us they were two *parures* old Lord Bloomfield had sent me as a present to wear at the Grand

Duchess Olga's wedding, which he thought I should have to attend.

We drove from Hamburg to Celle, and my delight was great when an old lady at one of the post-houses gave me a beautiful bouquet of roses. I suppose I testified it, much to her astonishment, for she asked me where I came from, and when I told her Russia, she opened her eyes, and looked at me almost as if I had been a bear. We visited the royal palace at Celle, where Queen Matilda, George the Second's unfortunate sister, was imprisoned. Her rooms are shown, and her picture, which is curiously like our Queen. The hair is much fairer, but the features are the same. The palace had lately been put into excellent repair by Ernest, King of Hanover, who occasionally visited Celle. His Majesty received us very kindly at Hanover, and wished us to stay there a day or two; but as we were in a hurry to reach home, we begged to be excused, but he received my husband, and kept him an hour and a half. The environs of Hanover are pretty and enjoyable. We dined with Mr. Bligh, and he drove us to see the mausoleum the King has lately erected for his wife's remains. For some years after her death he would not allow any change to be made in her establishment.

Her rooms were left exactly as they were when she died; at night candles were lighted, the pages and dressers were in attendance, and the King went regularly to pray at her bedside.

The King was very angry at the political state of affairs in England, and the abolition of the Corn Laws. He declared he was born an Englishman, and always had the interest of England much at heart, and he could not bear to witness the growth of Radicalism in his native land.

Whilst my husband had his audience, I visited the Palace, and saw the plate, which is very handsome. The Palace had lately been enlarged, and the King received there; but he resided in a small house opposite the Palace in some wretched small rooms on the ground floor. We left Hanover in the afternoon, slept at Bückeburg, where we drank tea with my old friend, Baroness Lehzen, who resided at Bückeburg with her sister in a comfortable small house, where she seemed perfectly contented and happy. She was as much devoted to the Queen as ever, and her rooms were filled with pictures and prints of Her Majesty. She told me that the Prince and Princess of Bückeburg were very kind to her, and she had as much society as she liked or required. I was very glad to see this remarkable woman again. She was always kind and friendly to me when I was a Maid of Honour, and I had a great regard for her. We reached London without misadventure, after a long and very hot journey.

Extracts of Letters written to my Husband (1846), *who returned to St. Petersburg for the Grand Duchess Olga's Marriage, leaving me in England:—*

14 *Portman Square, July* 1, 1846.—I have been sitting with your father, and read Psalm ciii. and chapter xiv. of St. John to him. He remarked upon their great beauty, and the consolation they conveyed. He was, if possible, more dear and kind than ever, and repeated what he said the first time he saw me after we were engaged, that he never remembers the day when you had done what he could have wished undone, or left undone what he wished done. How few fathers could put their hand on their heart and say the like! and surely I, as a wife, must deeply feel the blessing of having such a husband and such a father-in-law. It is such a comfort being able really to love one's husband's

relations as much as I can yours. All so kind, and so truly excellent. Your dear mother is as cheerful as ever, and so *very* comical. This morning she was taking off a man she once saw at the Pavilion, who had St. Vitus's dance, and she nearly killed us with laughing.

Sydney Lodge, July 13, 1846.—We dined last night with Mrs. Webber at Hamble Cliff. She is a pretty widow, the sister of the Bishop of Salisbury's first wife. We had a pleasant party, and I sat next Captain Hornby, R.N., who told me he lived near Woolwich, and knows you and your father. He has lately returned from the coast of Africa, and gave me a dreadful account of the coast fever; and also of the slave ships—three of which he captured. The fever was quite as severe in his ship as it was in the *Éclair;* out of nine officers who left England a year ago, he and one Lieutenant are the only survivors, and the number of men who have died is shocking. It is little short of murder sending our ships out there; and it seems that our present mode, instead of putting down the slave trade, only increases its horrors tenfold. For instead of the slave ships having proper accommodation for the poor creatures, they are built with the sole view of secrecy and speed; the consequence is, that out of four hundred and fifty thousand slaves who annually leave Africa, not more than one-fourth reach their destination. I am afraid to say the size of the cabin which contained three hundred and fifty slaves in the ship he captured, but I think it was thirty feet long, eighteen wide, and only two feet eight inches high, so that a man could hardly sit upright in it. The ship had only been twenty-four hours at sea when she was captured; but Captain Hornby said, that though he is not squeamish, the state of filth in the slave cabin was so dreadful that he was obliged to leave it instantly, and was nearly sick when he got on deck.

14 *Portman Square, July* 19, 1846.—Hardwicke arrived at Sydney Lodge from Plymouth on Friday, but he had a narrow escape in the *Susan*. He could not purchase either an anchor or cable at Plymouth for love or money, and being anxious not to disappoint Susan (my sixth sister, the Countess of Hardwicke), he very rashly left Plymouth without either in a gale of wind. It blew very hard on Thursday, but he would not put in to Dartmouth or any of the other ports on the coast, but made a run for Portland. The night was pitch dark, blowing a hurricane, with violent gusts of wind and rain—the sea mountains high;

and he declares that for about two hours he expected to founder every minute. The fatigue and anxiety were very great; and when at last, by God's mercy, he got into comparatively smooth water off Portland, from not having an anchor he was obliged to keep tacking all night, steering between the vessels, which were there in great numbers; and when he reached Sydney Lodge at two P.M. on Friday he had not left the helm for thirty-two hours, and was so dead beat he could hardly stand or speak. Susan luckily was spared great anxiety, for seeing how bad the weather was we all gave him credit for being prudent, and thought he would put into port till the gale subsided. His old servant, John Butler, who was many years at sea, said to his wife, 'Well, I only hope my lord has not started, for if he *is* out in an open boat on such a night as this he can never weather it!' Luckily the boat was a very fine one, and never shipped a drop of water.

Dyrham Park, Thursday, July 27, 1846.—I went with Lady Canning to a concert at Lansdowne House last night, which I enjoyed very much. The music was beautiful; and I saw heaps of people I like, all of whom seemed really glad to see me again, which was pleasant. They all looked rather as if I was Banquo's ghost, but nevertheless greeted me heartily. I sat next Lady Palmerston, and had a long chat with her. She assured me she did not believe there is any question of your being moved from St. Petersburg. Lord Westmoreland stays at Berlin and Sir Robert Gordon remains at Vienna for the present. Lady Waterford was looking more perfectly lovely than ever. I think she is the handsomest creature I ever saw, and so nice. Those two sisters (Charlotte, Viscountess Canning, and Louisa, Marchioness of Waterford, the daughters of Lord Stuart de Rothesay) are so genuine and charming; and Lady Waterford's late drawings are full of talent, and beautiful both in colour and design.

Extracts of Letters from my Husband.

St. Petersburg, July 12.—I have just returned from the Palace, and the ceremony went off beautifully. We assembled in a room adjoining the Chapel, and the company passed close by, so I had innumerable greetings from all sides. When all was ready, we, the *Chefs de Mission*, advanced to the Chapel, and took up our position to the right, headed by the Marshal, Prince Paskewitch, and the Ministers of State. Then came the Chamberlains and officers of the Court, and then the Imperial family. The bride looked lovely, but deadly pale; she was dressed in a white dress of course, embroidered in silver, and a diamond crown. The Prince of Wurtemberg (the bride-groom) seemed very nervous, and as the ceremony was very long, it must have been trying. The Emperor (Nicholas) was even more magnificent than usual, and I was rejoiced to see the Empress look composed and better than I expected. The Grand Duchesses Czarewna and Marie each had their eldest daughters with them, and the children behaved admirably. It was altogether a very fine sight, and I am sorry, for many reasons, that you were not present at it. Many honours have been conferred to-day, the sun shone brightly, the artillery did their duty well, and loud and long was the cheering of the thousands assembled in the garden, who had a good sight of the happy couple. As for the Grand Duchess Olga, she really surpassed herself in beauty, and her whole demeanour was so easy and natural, that it was most striking.

Peterhof, July 15, 1846.—We sallied forth about one o'clock to see the Parade and the Empress review the Chevalier Guards. The Emperor looked splendid, and went through all the forms of an officer commanding a regiment, which the Empress was inspecting. The usual evolutions took place, and after the Empress, who was accompanied by the bride and her sister, the Grand Duchess Marie of Leuchtenberg, and the Czarewna, had gone round the hollow square, she went to a window in the Palace, as unfortunately the rain came down most inopportunely. The two young Grand Dukes, Nicholas and Michael, are made cavalry officers, and had to go through the duties of orderly officers and soldiers, to the great satisfaction of the Emperor and Empress.

At eight we proceeded to the ball, and before dancing began we were presented to the bride and bridegroom. She looked most beautiful, in a rose crape gown, which was perfection, and was most amiable to me, saying everything that it was possible to say about my having returned here for her marriage. After the ball, we all drove out in *lignes* (*chars-à-bancs*), to see the illuminations, which were really splendid, and the water-works magnificent. Do you recollect a piece of water in front of the Palace? Round this there were rows of lamps, and then illuminated temples, bouquets, and trees of various coloured lamps, a boat with blue lights, showing the outline of it, perpetually moving on the lake, bands playing in the grounds;

in fact, one might have fancied oneself in fairy-land, realising some wonderful scene in the 'Arabian Nights.' To crown all, the night was lovely—perfectly still and sufficiently dark to give the illuminations their full *éclat*. The sky was of an Italian blue, the dancing was gay, and the humour of all the folk good. I am still in all the bewilderment of the scene, and doubt much if I shall ever again witness anything so beautiful. I cannot but deeply regret that you were not present. The crowd was awful, and as I had never before mixed with the public in this way, I was much amused.

The Emperor was *most gracious*; I never was spoken to by him in a tone of such kindness, and his acknowledgment of my father's desire that I should return here for this occasion was really beautiful.

Lieut.-General Lord Bloomfield was seriously ill at this time, which was the reason of our having returned to England, and my being absent from the marriage of the Grand Duchess Olga.

My husband went back to St. Petersburg alone, leaving me in Portman Square with his father, but returned in time to attend his death-bed. He died peacefully on August 15, 1846, and was buried at Loughton, King's Co. We went to

Ireland for a short time, and returned to Russia in the autumn.

October 8, 1846.—We left London on our return to St. Petersburg, but made a little *détour* by Belgium and the Rhine, visiting Antwerp, where we were greatly delighted with Rubens' *chef d'œuvres*—the 'Elevation of the Cross' and the 'Descent from the Cross,' in the Cathedral, though they were unfortunately so badly lighted it was difficult to see them. At Bonn we met Count Bjornsterna, an old friend of my husband's, then, I think, Swedish Minister in London. He took us to see his sister, who was the Lady Superior of the Hospital, attached to the Palace at Bonn. Having had a disappointment in early life, when the gentleman she was engaged to marry died, she determined to devote the rest of her life to charity and good works. She lived in a little room very like a cell, and spent all her time in nursing the sick and conducting the large establishment of which she was head. A bright, cheerful old lady, who seemed to reap the reward of the path she had chosen, by being at peace with God and man.

The weather was very fine, and we greatly enjoyed our drive up the right bank of the Rhine. We stopped to see Stolzenfels, where the King of

Prussia received the Queen in 1845. It is beautifully situated on a high rock overhanging the river, and the interior was well fitted up. Part of the old castle remains, but has been so well restored it is not to be distinguished from the modern part of the building. We spent one day at Frankfort, then visited Aschaffenburg, where there is a very fine palace belonging to the King of Bavaria. Princess Reuss told me the following strange story about her aunt, the late Queen Theresa, of Bavaria. It appears that in the Bavarian Royal family, there is a tradition of the appearance of a black lady before any death ; just as in the Prussian Royal family a white lady is seen. One evening, Queen Theresa was sitting with her brother, on the eve of her departure for Munich, when her lady-in-waiting came into Her Majesty's room, and asked whether she was going to give an audience, because though she, the lady-in-waiting, had not been apprised of that intention, a lady was waiting in the ante-room ! The Queen, much astonished, said she had no intention of seeing anyone that evening, as she meant to start very early the next morning for Munich, and wished to retire to rest in good time. Her Majesty then asked her brother to go and see the lady in question, and inquire what she wanted. On entering the ante-room, he saw the figure dressed in black, sitting; but as he approached it disappeared, so he came back to the Queen and said, 'Es ist sehr unheimlich, es muss die Schwarze Frau gewesen seyn' (it is very uncanny, but it must have been the black lady). The next morning, at 6 A.M., the Queen started for Munich. As she was leaving Aschaffenburg, she told her chaplain she had left various petitions on her writing table, which she wished him to attend to, and as soon as the carriage drove off he went to get the papers, and there, standing by the Queen's table, was again the same figure dressed in black. That evening, after the Castellan and his wife had retired to rest, they were surprised at hearing the great bell of the Castle toll. The key of the bell tower was hanging up as usual in their room; but they noted the hour, and at that moment Queen Theresa died at Munich of cholera, which seized her on her arrival in the town at 6 P.M., and carried her off in a few hours.

> I know not how the truth may be,
> I tell the tale as 'twas told to me.

Wurzburg is an interesting and very picturesque old town. The Dom Kirche is very fine. As it was the Queen of Bavaria's name day, and a high festival, the church was filled with officers in full uniform, and a great crowd attended high mass. The priests were splendidly attired, the music was very fine, and the whole scene most striking. The old fortress, which crowns the hill above the town, commands a magnificent view of Wurzburg and the Main. The place was besieged by the Swedes during the Thirty Years' War, and one of their cannon balls may still be seen imbedded in the wall. The church is said to have been originally a temple built by the Romans, and dedicated to the Goddess Diana. It contains a number of relics; among others, a thorn from our Lord's crown is contained in a fine gold and crystal cup, which is 300 years old, and was brought from Rome. The Royal Palace is very large. The Queen slept there one night on her way to Coburg; but in general it is not inhabited, though kept in very good repair. The staircase is extremely handsome, the rooms very numerous. It was built and inhabited by the Prince Bishops of Wurzburg, and is not above 120 years old. The cellars are enormous, and celebrated for the Steinberg wine, which belongs exclusively to the King.

Bamberg is another interesting old town, especially the Rathhaus, where there are some curious frescoes on the outer walls. The Cathedral is chiefly remarkable from two distinct styles of architecture—the Byzantine and the Gothic. It is very simple, but the proportions of its massive pillars and the great height of the groined roof make it striking, and reminded me of one of our own fine Gothic cathedrals. The crypts are curious, and were used for divine service very early in the thirteenth century. We spent a day at Nüremberg, visited the famous Lorenz and St. Sebaldus churches, which are very fine, and contain some interesting sculpture. There are also some very good pictures to be seen, especially some Albert Dürers. The house where he resided is still shown. Altogether, Nüremberg is the most picturesque town in Germany; some of the houses have inner courts and stone balconies, which are very ornamental.

At Berlin I made the acquaintance of H.R.H. the Princess of Prussia. She received me most kindly, showed me her Palace, which was very pretty, and from that day never varied in her friendship towards us, which she testified on many occasions—a friendship I value very much, and which added greatly to the pleasure of our residence at Berlin from 1851 to 1860.

We dined with Lord and Lady Westmoreland at Berlin, and went to a party at M. Antonini's, the Neapolitan Minister, where we had the pleasure of hearing Countess Rossi, *née* Sontag, sing. Her voice was as fresh and beautiful as ever, and nothing could be more perfect than her style. I believe she always regretted having left the stage, and she returned to it some years later, and died whilst on a professional tour in America. She had magnificent light hair, and once when she was singing with Pasta in 'Otello,' the latter in the last scene seized her by the hair, and dragged her across the stage. Poor Sontag shrieked with pain, but the audience thought she was acting splendidly, and applauded enthusiastically!

We returned to St. Petersburg on November 4, 1846, and on the 6th I was presented to old Countess Nesselrode, *née* Gourieff. She was very kind to me, but was rather an alarming woman, with brusque manners, and I was not a little astonished at seeing her hold out her pocket handkerchief by the corners, and spit into the middle of it! She smoked a great deal, but was clever and agreeable, and talked pleasantly.

On Monday, January $\frac{6}{17}$, 1847, I went to the Winter Palace to witness the ceremony of the blessing of the Neva, which takes place every year at the Feast of Epiphany. I had a very good place in a window immediately opposite the chapel, which is erected on the ice over the spot where a hole is made and the cross is immersed. The ceremony began by a procession of Priests, Bishops, Archbishops, Archimandrite, and lastly, the Metropolitan. The Priests walked two and two, carrying banners, candles, and lastly, an immense cross. They then formed in a triple line on each side of the way to the chapel, which was covered with crimson cloth. Then the Emperor came out attended by the Grand Dukes Héritier and Michael, and all the General Officers, Aides-de-camp, and Court in full uniform, and bareheaded. The Czar walked to the chapel, and stood there whilst mass was performed and the cross immersed, after which he went forward and kissed the Metropolitan's hand, who blessed him, and sprinkled him and the Grand Dukes with holy water. Then the procession returned in the same order in which it went; the Metropolitan dipped a sprig of rosemary in a cup which was carried before him, sprinkling all those who were fortunate enough to be within reach. The *coup d'œil* was very striking—such a vast multitude assembled to witness the ceremony; and at the moment the cross was immersed the fortress guns fired and the crowd uncovered their heads in one instant.

The greatest order prevailed, but there was a tremendous rush as soon as the ceremony was over, and the last priest had left the chapel. The water is put into barrels, and sent off to the various great churches in Russia, and sometimes women dip their babies in the hole, and believe, if the poor infants die, that they go straight to heaven! The Empress was too unwell to attend the ceremony, so none of the Court ladies were present. Fortunately, there were only three degrees of frost, which was very unusual at that season of the year; but, however severe the weather, the Czar always attends the ceremony bareheaded, and in full uniform, without a cloak.

I was asking General Berg one day how the troops could stand the extreme cold, and he told me that when they are kept standing very long during the great winter parades some soldiers are almost always frozen. He said the most intense cold he ever experienced was once in the reign of the Emperor Alexander, when he was out in full uniform from three A.M. till four P.M. in 26° of frost Réaumur. This was on the occasion of the reception of a Persian Ambassador, and the road for several versts was lined with troops. His Excellency rode on an elephant, and the poor beast had to wear fur shoes, and sometimes when one of these dropped off the whole procession stopped, and the animal put its foot out to have its shoe replaced.

Friday, January 28, 1847.—I received a note from Count Nesselrode to inform me that the Empress would receive me at the Winter Palace at half-past eight that evening. Her Majesty had had the influenza, and therefore my presentation was to be quite private, and I was to wear a plain evening dress without a train. On arriving at the Winter Palace I was immediately shown up to the Empress's apartments, where I was received by two friends, Countess Julie Bobrinsky, maid of honour in waiting, and Prince Michael Kotchubey. Soon after Madame Baranoff, the Grande Maîtresse, arrived, and took me to the Empress's boudoir, where Her Majesty received me. She was seated when I went in, but rose to meet me, and then desired me to sit down beside her. She looked very thin, but not so ill as I expected, and her face bore the traces of great refinement and beauty. Her eyes, which were blue, were set deep in her head, and the expression was more intelligent than pleasing. Her voice was soft, but she spoke rapidly and with decision. Her Majesty was dressed in a plain black velvet gown made high and with long sleeves. She wore a small coquettish black hat and feather, which was fastened by a handsome diamond aigrette, and she had on a magnificent pearl necklace composed of five rows, each pearl as large as a hazel nut, which rested on her knees as she was sitting. I remained about half an hour with Her Majesty, who talked a great deal on various subjects. I mentioned that I had lately received a letter from the Queen; this seemed to astonish her not a little, and she said, 'Comment donc, mais de sa vraie propre main! Est-il possible que la Reine ait le temps d'écrire des lettres!' The Empress admired the Queen's activity, and said the Emperor had been so much struck by it, and that she believed that Queen Victoria and the Queen of Greece were the only two female sovereigns who occupied themselves so much, mind and body. The Empress also spoke much and most kindly of my dear friend, Countess Sophie Bobrinsky; then she suddenly asked me when the Queen was to open Parliament. I answered that Her Majesty had already done so, in the beginning of last week; 'but,' the Empress rejoined, 'the Speech has not arrived;' and she seemed surprised when I mentioned that my husband had received it that morning from Count Nesselrode. The Empress asked me what it contained, and what the Queen had said about the Montpensier marriage? I thought the conversation was then touching delicate subjects, and that the annexation of Cracow to the Austrian dominions would be the next topic, so, 'as prudence is the better part of valour,' I said, to tell the honest truth, I had not read the Speech myself, as it arrived just at the moment I received Her Majesty's summons, and I was more taken up with the thoughts of my audience than I was with the Speech. Her Majesty laughed, and said, 'Oh c'était bien comme une jeune femme!' and I was content to get out of the scrape with this gentle reproof. Her Majesty had got a beautiful little English spaniel, which attracted my admiration, and I was amused at hearing her say to it, 'Oh, you young rascal!' When I took leave she said, 'Eh bien! nous nous sommes vues à la fin, mais Dieu sait quand nous nous reverrons.' I could not but think that possibly it might be my first and last interview, for Her Majesty's health was so sadly delicate everything was an effort to her, and she seldom appeared in public; but I had many more opportunities of seeing her, and she lived till the year 1860, outliving her husband by five years.

February, 1847.—I went to a morning concert

to hear the Moscow gipsies sing. There were about twelve women and six men, not dressed as I had expected in their national costumes, but in tawdry, dirty finery, with wreaths and toques upon their heads. They looked disgustingly impudent, and nothing could exceed the savage wildness of their singing. The airs were national and very pretty, and occasionally when they sang piano the effect was pleasing; but the screaming, shrieking, and roaring of the choruses was deafening. They got excessively excited, flung their limbs about, and banged the guitars with which they accompanied themselves. What struck me most was that although the din was so great that it was next to impossible to follow the melody, they all sang in perfect time, and kept their parts well. The music would have been much more pleasing in the open air. The women were all handsome, and had, without exception, beautiful expressive black eyes and lovely hands; but otherwise they were very coarse, and most of them were middle-aged and *passée*.

March 6th.—We went to a party at Princess Yousoupoff's fine palace. At the top of the staircase there was a garden and a fountain playing, which almost made one forget the want of external vegetation. The Princess's jewels were exposed to view in glass cases. Her pearls and diamonds were very fine indeed, and she possessed one called the Pérégrine, which alone was valued at 6000*l.* It was very large, pear-shaped, and formed the drop of an earring.

March 9.—We attended Prince Vassiltchikoff's funeral, which was performed in the Strass-Préobrajensky Church. The deceased was President of the Council of the Empire, Aide-de-camp Général, and a man universally esteemed and regretted—a personal friend of the Emperor. When we arrived the church was quite full. The Corps Diplomatique attended in full uniform, and the sight was very striking. The coffin was on a raised catafalque in the middle of the church. The body, dressed in full uniform, was in a sitting posture, and covered with a cloth of gold pall; but the head was exposed and looked very ghastly, and the expression extremely painful. The female relatives stood on the right, the Emperor, Hereditary Grand Duke, and the male relatives on the left side of the coffin, and all round it were velvet cushions, with the various decorations of the deceased. The service was performed by a number of priests, headed by the Metropolitan, and lasted about an hour and a half. The priests wore black velvet copes embroidered in silver, and every one present held a taper; six large tapers burnt round the coffin. Towards the conclusion of the ceremony, the Metropolitan read a paper, containing the Prince's profession of faith and declaration that he died an orthodox member of the Greek Church. This paper was placed in the hands of the corpse, then the relatives went up one by one to kiss the hands and cheek of the deceased, and take their final leave of him, which was the most touching part of the whole ceremony. The body was then covered with wadding, and the coffin lid was put on. It was carried out of the church by the Czarewitch, the Duke of Leuchtenberg, and the different members of the Prince's family, and was to be interred at the family seat some hundred of versts distant. The Emperor accompanied the hearse to the Moscow Gate, and it was followed by a large file of cavalry, in spite of 20° of frost.

Saturday, March 13.—We were invited, with the rest of the Corps Diplomatique, to attend the christening of the Grand Duchess Marie of Leuchtenberg's second son, Prince Eugene Maximilianôwitch, which took place in the chapel of the Winter Palace. We assembled at half-past ten in full Court dress, and at eleven the Emperor and Empress arrived, followed by their four sons, the Czarewitch, Grand Dukes Constantine, Nicholas, and Michael, the Duke of Leuchtenberg, the Grand Duke Michael, the Duke of Oldenburg and the whole Court. The effect at that moment was most striking, the chapel gorgeous with gilding, and the splendour of the dresses was the finest *coup d'œil* I ever witnessed. The Empress was dressed in a robe of cloth of gold, trimmed with ermine, and wore three rows of large diamonds on her red velvet kakoschkine. This is a semi-circular diadem, from which hangs a long veil, and is the characteristic of the Russian Court dress. The ladies-in-waiting and maids of honour were all dressed alike—in velvet trains embroidered in gold—except that the ladies wore green, the maids of honour crimson. The dress was very handsome, the petticoats were white satin embroidered in gold, some of the kakoschkines were ornamented with jewels, but generally they were plain, with a row of pearls top and bottom. Madame Zacharjewsky, the lady-in-waiting to the Grand Duchess Marie, carried the infant immediately after the Emperor and Empress. I had an excellent place next the rail, which divided the chapel into two parts, and within which no one stood except the Imperial family. The ceremony was performed by the

Metropolitan, attended by two other high dignitaries of the Greek Church and about ten priests. Their vestments were magnificent, silver tissue with a pattern of crimson velvet, and the Metropolitan's mitre was covered with jewels. The Emperor and his grandchild, the Grand Duchess Marie's eldest girl, were sponsors, and each carried tapers. The baby was stripped, and completely immersed in holy water, and was afterwards wrapped up in wadding covered with cambric, and then rolled in a white mantle. As soon as the christening was over mass was said, after which the Empress, supported on one side by the Emperor and on the other by the Czarewitch, carried the baby up to the Metropolitan, who administered to it the Holy Communion. This singular custom is, I believe, peculiar to the Greek Church, in which children of all ages are communicants. The Emperor then invested the infant with the order and ribbon of St. Michael. The Duke of Leuchtenberg being a Roman Catholic was not present during the christening; but he came as soon as it was over, and embraced his relatives, and received their congratulations. The ceremony lasted till one o'clock, when the Court retired in the order in which it arrived; the sun was then shining brightly, and the play of light upon the rich dresses was strikingly beautiful as the procession marched through the State apartments, which were lined with troops.

Saturday, April 3.—Being Easter Eve I went with Countess Julie Strogonoff to the midnight mass at the Winter Palace. Neither the Emperor nor the Empress were able to attend it. I was allowed to go to a gallery, which commanded a view of the chapel. The body of the church was completely filled with officers of State and the whole Court in full dress. As soon as the Czarewitch and other members of the Imperial family appeared, the service began by the choristers heading a procession, followed by the priests, who carried the icons, and these were followed by the Imperial family. After having traversed the principal apartments the procession re-entered the chapel, and vespers began. Soon after midnight the Metropolitan left the altar bearing a gold jewelled crucifix, with which he first made the sign of the cross, and then presented it to the Czarewitch, who kissed it, and then embraced the Metropolitan on both cheeks. The priests wore the same gorgeous vestments they had on at the christening, and each carried either a folio bound in gold and inlaid with pictures, or else an icon. The Czarewitch approached each and kissed them, as he had done the Metropolitan, and he was followed by the Grand Duchess Marie and the rest of the Imperial family. When the Emperor comes to the ceremony he is embraced by all present from the first to the last, and this takes several hours; but as this is only an act of fealty to the reigning sovereign it did not take place in his absence, but as soon as the Imperial family returned to their places mass was said. People congratulated each other on Christ being risen, and much embracing went on; but I retired about two o'clock before the service was quite over. The chapel was brilliantly illuminated, and the *coup d'œil* was very fine indeed. When the Bible was read the Metropolitan stood at the altar within the doors; but three other reading desks were placed at the different sides of the chapel, and the priests read from them alternately, which typified the preaching of the Gospel throughout the world!

CHAPTER IX.

The Islands—Visits to the Emperor and Empress at Peterhof, and the camp at Krasnoe Selo.

June 8 (17 N.S.), 1847.—We moved out to the Strogonoff Datcha at the Islands. The weather was still cold, and the leaves only just beginning to come out; but the Islands are pretty in the summer, the houses all decorated with a profusion of flowers and evergreens, and when the Court visits Jelaguine, where there is a small Palace, the Islands are very gay and animated. There was a band of music every evening at Jelaguine, and the Emperor, driving the Empress in a little open pony carriage, came every evening to listen to it. The day the Court went away the Islands seemed almost deserted, and though the weather was very fine, we scarcely met a soul driving. When once vegetation begins the progress it makes is so rapid, it reminded me of the tale of Jack's bean-stalk, which grew up in one night. I literally could sometimes hear the buds

cracking, and the wild flowers were very pretty; many of them were new to me. The white orchis, called 'Belle de nuit,' which grew luxuriantly, in some places was deliciously sweet, and the wormwood smelt very fragrant in the pine woods in summer. The lilies of the valley were plentiful, and the finest I ever saw.

Tuesday, June 15.—Count Nesselrode paid us a visit, and told me the Emperor intended inviting us to Peterhof; on Thursday we received a summons from Count Schouvaloff inviting us for the following Saturday, and saying the Empress would receive us that evening. This we expected would be conclusive, but on Saturday morning a Feld jäger arrived at half-past ten o'clock to say we were to dine at the Empress's cottage that day at four o'clock, so we started as soon as possible, and arrived in time. The Emperor and Empress received us most graciously and kindly, and both expressed their pleasure at being able to receive us *en famille*. The party was very small, Madame Baranoff and Mademoiselle Nélidoff being the only ladies besides myself. When dinner was announced, the Empress walked into the dining-room by herself; the Emperor gave me his arm, and placed me next himself, the Empress being on his other side, and my husband next Her

Majesty. Nothing could have been less formal or pleasanter than the dinner; their Majesties both talked a great deal, and during dinner the Czare-witch's two eldest children, and their two cousins, the Grand Duchess Marie's, came into the room and played about. It was charming to see the Emperor and Empress's manner with their children and grandchildren; it was so very kind and affectionate, and the little ones were as merry and playful as possible. During dinner the Emperor told me the great delight it gave him and the Empress to live quietly at their cottage, which was given to the Empress by the Emperor Alexander just before his departure to the Crimea, where he died. It had been a favourite spot of the Empress's, and she chose it in preference to any other; and when the Emperor Alexander gave her the ground, she sent for an old English archi-tect, who had been sixty years in Russia, who made the plan of the cottage. Before the addition of the dining-room, it consisted of five rooms only on the ground floor—a room to the right of the entrance, the drawing-room facing the sea, next that the Empress's boudoir, bed-room and dressing-room. The Emperor's room was on the first floor over the dining-room, and commanded a beautiful view of Cronstadt on one side, and St. Petersburg on the other. The other rooms were occupied by the Imperial family, and the Emperor told me he had lived for several years with his wife, four children, and two servants, and regretted exceedingly when his increasing family, and obligations as Emperor, obliged him to enlarge the house a little by building a dining-room, 'quand' (to use his own words) 'il a fallu sortir de notre modestie. Ce n'etait que le hasard, madame,' he added, 'qui m'a fait monter le trône, auparavant nous vivions très-modestement; maintenant, tout en remplissant les obligations de notre haute position, je vous assure que nous conservons toujours nos goûts simples. Nous aimons surtout ce séjour que nous devons à la bonté de mon Frère, qui nous l'a donné quand nous n'avions pas un coin de terre, et je puis dire en vérité que tout ce que vous voyez a été créé par ma femme.'

When dinner was over, and we had adjourned to the drawing-room, the Empress said she must show me her private apartments herself. She took me into her sitting-room, bed-room, and dressing-room, and then into the garden. We went all round the cottage, and Her Majesty re-entered by a different door from that she went out at, to the no small surprise of her attendants, who did not expect to see us arrive on that side.

The Empress was amused at their astonishment. She then took leave of us, and invited us to drive with her at seven o'clock. We returned to our apartments in the 'Grand Palais,' where I changed my dress, and at seven we went back to the cottage. The Empress got into her little pony carriage, and invited Lord Bloomfield to sit next her, whilst I sat next the Emperor, who drove. The young Grand Dukes followed in their pony carriage, and the attendants in a third. We drove through the gardens, where the fountains were playing beautifully; the sun shone brightly, and the fresh green of the foliage made everything look gay and cheerful. The Emperor pointed out several improvements he had been making, and seemed to take the greatest interest in the place. I took an opportunity of expressing to His Majesty my great regret that my dear father-in-law's illness had obliged us to return home the previous year, and prevented my attending the Grand Duchess Olga's marriage. He said he too had regretted my absence, and especially the cause of it; for that he had the greatest regard and highest esteem for my father-in-law, who was one of his oldest friends, he having known him when he visited George IV. in 1814, and that he had always entertained a great friendship for him. I said I had often heard the late Lord Bloomfield speak with the warmest gratitude of his Imperial Majesty's kindness not only towards himself but towards his son, upon which the Emperor said, 'Oh, quant à votre mari, madame, il est si bon et si estimable qu'il serait impossible de le connaître sans l'aimer et l'estimer, et nous nous sentons heureux de l'avoir en Russie.'

After driving for about an hour and a half, we arrived at the Isola Bella, where tea was prepared. It is a beautiful little spot, fitted up like an Italian villa, the walls painted in the Etruscan style, and the rooms supported by marble pillars. The Empress was very fond of it, and frequently went there. It was full of flowers, and reminded one of Italy. I could not help smiling when I thought under what a different aspect I saw the Island then, to when I had crossed over, as a tourist, in the rickety flower raft the preceding summer. After tea we drove again, but the Grand Duchess Marie, who had joined the party, took my husband's place next the Empress. We drove to Znamenska, and I was shown into a private room, where I found my maid, and arranged my dress for the evening. The Court had all been invited to spend the evening at Znamenska, and it went off very gaily. There were *petits-jeux*, but the

Empress expressed a wish to hear me sing, and had had her own pianoforte brought from the cottage for that purpose. Nothing could have exceeded her kindness to me. She said how much she regretted that the delicate state of her health had prevented her seeing me oftener during the winter, that she had made a great effort to receive me, which had given her the wish to see me again, and that she was delighted to have us as her guests at Peterhof. She called me to her table at supper, and treated me with the greatest condescension and distinction. It was midnight when we returned to the Palace.

On Sunday morning there was mass, which we did not attend, and then a parade. The Empress sent to desire that I would join her on the balcony, where luncheon was served, but Her Majesty did not remain very long, as she was fatigued. The parade, which the Emperor attended, was interesting, and I was especially struck by the picturesque appearance of the Circassians. A piece of paper was fastened to the ground, and each man shot at it as he galloped past, till it was rent in pieces. At four o'clock there was a dinner of 100 people at the Grand Palais. The Emperor sat between the Empress and the Grand Duchess Marie, whilst I was placed next the Grand Duke Michael, who sat on the Empress's left. After dinner the Empress said she was aware that no amusements are allowed in England on Sunday; but she begged me nevertheless to attend the theatre that evening, as she wished to see me again. Between the acts the Emperor came himself to fetch me, and took me to a room where I found the Empress and the Grand Duchess Marie at tea. There the Empress took leave of me, the Emperor conducting me back to the box.

After the play, Julie Bobrinsky proposed driving with me in an open carriage to hear the nightingales, which abound in the environs of Peterhof. It was quite light, the weather was delightful, not a leaf was stirring, and the still waters of the gulf were like a mirror. We drove along the shore from 'Mon Plaisir' to a new pavilion, which the Emperor built in imitation of one at Palermo, which His Majesty greatly admired. The nightingales were singing sweetly, and the night was so still, each note was distinctly heard. We stayed out for about a couple of hours, and enjoyed the drive extremely; but I could not help comparing the liberty of the maids of honour in Russia to that enjoyed at Windsor, and thinking how scandalised the Queen would have been had Her Majesty heard of our driving about the Park and visiting Virginia Water in the middle of the night! On Monday morning we called on Madame Baranoff, Countess Tiesenhausen, the Barténieffs, Julie Bobrinsky, Madame Schouvaloff, and Countess Razoumoffsky, and at one o'clock we went to pay our respects to the Grand Duchess Marie, at Serieffsky. She and the Duke of Leuchtenberg received us very kindly, and showed us all over the house and gardens. We lunched on the balcony, and then drove through the grounds. The place belonged to M. Narischkine, but was bought by the Emperor and given to the Grand Duchess when she married. Near the sea there is a little Roman Catholic chapel, which is the room where the Grand Duchess's eldest girl died. It was in another place, but was moved, and the Duke turned it into a chapel for himself, and built a Greek chapel for the Grand Duchess on the spot where it had stood. On leaving Serieffsky we returned home to the islands, having enjoyed our visit to Peterhof extremely.

Saturday, June 26.—We dined with our kind friends, Count and Countess Koucheleff, at their country house on the Peterhof road. The place was very enjoyable and well kept. The Count took great pains with his farm, and had some good English stock. On July 28, we went a large party to Pergola, a pretty place, belonging to Count Schouvaloff, about twenty versts from St. Petersburg. Differing from the surrounding country, the ground there is prettily undulated, and the timber is larger and finer than one usually sees. Princess Butera, Count Schouvaloff's mother, married first Count Schouvaloff, then a M. Pollier, and thirdly Prince Butera. Her two first husbands are buried at Pergola, and M. Pollier's tomb is in a beautiful little garden, which is kept with the greatest care. Some years previous to this date, my husband was Chargé d'Affaires at St. Petersburg, where Prince Butera called upon him, and offered to stay for dinner. Mr. Bloomfield said nothing would give him greater pleasure, only unfortunately he had already invited eleven guests, and that he knew there is a great objection to sitting down thirteen to dinner! Prince Butera laughed, and said, Oh! that was all nonsense, and he should come, which he did. Exactly the same thing occurred on another occasion, when he again came up from the country, and unexpectedly proposed staying to dinner; but it is a melancholy fact, that before the year was out he died, though apparently in the full vigour of health when he dined with my husband.

Thursday, July 29.—At six o'clock we received a letter from Count Orloff, to say the Emperor invited us to the camp at Krasnoe Selo, and hoped we should go there that evening, to be ready for the cavalry manœuvres on Friday morning. My husband started immediately, but I was unfortunately obliged to give up seeing the manœuvres, as I was indisposed; but I went to Krasnoe Selo the next morning, and arrived there about one. We were lodged in a small house, with our colleagues, Prince Hohenlohe and M. Nordin, the Wurtemberg and Swedish Ministers. Soon after my arrival the troops returned from their field-day, and it was a beautiful sight, the sun shining upon the cuirasses and standards of the Chevalier Guards, and lighting up the road as far as the eye could reach. Krasnoe Selo is a village situated upon an immense open down; the ground rises there considerably, and the place is admirably adapted for the manœuvres, which take place there every year, during about six weeks. The troops live in tents, and the air is so fine that, generally speaking, they are more healthy in camp than in their barracks. In the village there are a few small houses, which were occupied by the female members of the Imperial family and their suites, but the Emperor always lived in a tent.

We were invited to dine with the Grand Duchess Marie at four o'clock, as the Empress was unwell, and had not arrived; but her sister, Princess Louise of the Netherlands, and her daughter had accompanied the Grand Duchess to the camp, and we sat down twenty to dinner, which was as many as the small room would hold. Dinner lasted about an hour and a half, after which we returned to our apartments till seven, when we were summoned to attend the Imperial family, and just as we were starting, the Empress arrived, and went with us to the camp. The evening threatened to be rainy, and all round the horizon the rain seemed to be falling heavily; but it fortunately kept off, and the effect of the sun setting behind a heavy mass of clouds, lighting up the camp, which spread far and wide in all directions, and the brilliant uniforms of the soldiers, was very striking. Every evening the troops formed in line in front of their tents; all the bands belonging to the different regiments assembled in front of the Emperor's, and played till nine o'clock, when three rockets were sent off, the artillery fired on every side of the camp, the retreat was sounded, and the bands struck up the Evening Hymn. At that instant every helmet was doffed, and the troops made the sign of the cross, after which the

Lord's Prayer was repeated and then all retired to rest. The effect was the most electrical I ever witnessed before or since, and I never heard anything so grand as the Evening Hymn played by about 2,000 men. Altogether, the army at the camp amounted to 53,000 men.

As soon as we reached the camp, we went to the Emperor's tent, which was not much larger than the others, or in any way distinguishable. Tea was served there, after which the Empress got into her carriage, which took up its position opposite the bands. As the evening was fine the rest of the party remained on foot, and a good many people came from town to hear the retreat. The Emperor, as usual, was most kind and courteous to me. He shook me cordially by the hand, and said how happy he was to see me at the camp; and when I expressed my gratitude to His Majesty for his kindness, in allowing me to witness such a magnificent sight, he said that, on the contrary, he was much flattered at my taking the trouble to come, and he only hoped I should not be over fatigued.

The Emperor Nicholas certainly had the most winning chevaleresque manner I ever saw, and it was touching and charming to see his behaviour to the Empress: it was so attentive and affectionate, and at the same time so respectful. He looked magnificent, standing alone among the multitude, his grand head towering above them all, his figure so erect and commanding; no one could for an instant mistake him. As soon as the Lord's Prayer was concluded, the Emperor dismissed the troops, wished the Empress 'good night,' embraced his sons, and retired to his tent. The Empress returned to her tent, and I was invited alone to sup with Her Majesty. I sat next her all the evening, and conversed on many different subjects. Her conversation was easy and agreeable, and I thought Her Majesty looked better and younger than I had ever seen her. Her head always shook a little, and had done so since the day the Emperor ascended the throne in 1826, when there was an *émeute* at St. Petersburg, and he took the Grand Duke Héritier in his arms and showed him to the mob. This was such a shock to the Empress's nerves, she never really recovered it.

At nine o'clock on Saturday morning we all assembled again at the Empress's, and adjourned to a 'pavilion' of the Emperor's, in the garden, where, with the aid of an excellent telescope, we could perfectly distinguish and follow the manœuvres on the hill opposite. There was a feigned attack on the village of Krasnoe Selo, and the infantry forded a piece of water, which lay in a hollow between the camp and the village. I was amused at seeing one soldier who, after crossing the water, quietly sat down on a stone, turned up his dripping white trousers, pulled off his boots and emptied the water out of them, wrung out the rags the soldiers wore round their legs in lieu of stockings, and then, after quietly replacing these various articles, continued his march.

About eleven we drove with the Empress to a different part of the camp, where her tent was pitched, where we stayed whilst Her Majesty drove with her sister and the Grand Duchess Marie to inspect the troops. On her return the infantry and artillery performed various evolutions, and then luncheon was served. The Empress desired me to sit next her, and told me to help myself without ceremony, adding that 'one must not be particular, *en temps de guerre*.' Presently a young aide-de-camp of the Emperor's arrived, with a message about the movement of the troops, and the Empress thanked him *en le tutoyant*. She then laughingly turned to me, and said, 'I must explain this to Lady Bloomfield, or else, if she writes a memoir she would say, "I was surprised to hear the Empress of Russia '*tutoyer*' *all* the

Emperor's aide-de-camps."' I laughed, and said, 'Ce serait bien une histoire de voyageuse, Madame!' which amused the Empress, who, nevertheless, went on to explain the circumstance by saying, that one or two young men had been brought up and educated with the Hereditary Grand Duke, and that she a'ways looked upon them almost as her sons, and not only *tutoyé'd* them, but generally embraced them into the bargain.

The young officer in question was Count Apraxine, and the Empress further showed her goodwill towards him by giving him a good luncheon, which he fully appreciated. A violent thunderstorm brought the exercises to an end sooner than was expected, so we returned to our home and dined alone. At seven we went to a cottage of the Empress's, at Doudouroff, about four miles from Krasnoe Selo, where the Court assembled for tea. The cottage was prettily situated at the top of a wooded hill; it was built in the Swiss style, and the Empress told me she was very fond of it, as it was exactly like a favourite residence of her aunt, Princess William of Prussia, in Silesia. A large party assembled, for, besides the Court, most of the general officers had been invited. Unfortunately, so much rain had fallen we were not able to see the walks, which looked pretty. The cottage was surrounded by peasants in their picturesque dresses, who carried plates of wild fruits and flowers, which they offered for sale. The scene was very pretty, and the Empress commemorated the evening by making us all write our names in a book which she kept for that purpose. From Doudouroff we drove back to the camp, and to reach the Emperor's tent, we had to drive from one end of it to the other. The soldiers were in line, but in each regiment a group was singing, with one man in the middle of it dancing. The men's voices sounded very harmonious, as they were singing their national melodies in parts, and the effect was striking and good. When we arrived at the spot where the band was stationed, the Emperor left the Empress's carriage, and came to fetch me, saying, 'Ma femme vous prie de venir prendre ma place.' He then ordered our carriage to drive alongside the Empress's, in order that I might not wet my feet, opened the carriage door himself, and handed me out. I remained with the Empress till after the retreat, the Emperor leaning on the carriage door, talking to us most familiarly, and I drove back with Her Majesty to Krasnoe Selo, where she took a most kind and gracious leave of me, shook my hand, and wished me adieu. We left the camp immediately, and reached home about two o'clock in the morning, our return having been delayed by the breaking of the axletree of our carriage. The accident happened about two versts from Mr. Anderson's country house, so we got assistance there, and he gave us the means of returning home.

General Count Berg, Aide-de-Camp General, and a distinguished officer, who had served in Turkey, told me that on one occasion he had been selected by the Emperor to command the army which was to be beaten at one of the sham fights, which take place at the manœuvres. Being an old and experienced officer, he determined to do his best to avoid this catastrophe, so, a few days before the fight, he went down and examined the ground carefully, and when the day arrived he made such a skilful retreat, that he and his men were not forthcoming, and could not be found. The Emperor was furious, and the next day he sent for General Count Berg, gave him a severe reprimand, and told him he should never be employed again, which was, in fact, exactly what the Count wished, as he was getting old, and did not care for the work. He, however, defended his case, told the Emperor that in real warfare it would have been the right course to pursue, and he could not regret what, as a military man, he felt was right. The Empress had arranged a ball at Gatchina, which was a failure, owing to the lack of officers, and this perhaps had added to the Emperor's annoyance.

Once, at a review my husband attended, an officer in command made an egregious mistake, by leading his men up a hill in the face of a strong force of artillery, which was blazing away at them. The Emperor's quick eye speedily detected the error, and, in a perfect fury, he drew his sword and rode at the wretched officer in command, and my husband said he hardly knew what would happen, but thought the Emperor was going to cut off the culprit's épaulettes. After, however, giving him a severe reprimand, the Emperor turned round to the suite, and said 'Gentlemen, after the humiliating spectacle we have just witnessed, I think the review had better conclude, so adieu;' and he turned his horse's head, and galloped off the field.

CHAPTER X.

Finland—Moscow — Churches — Imperial Palace—The Sparrow Hills — Foundling Hospital — Troitzka — Archangliska — Melnitza—Novgorod.

August 14–26, 1847.—We left the islands at 6 P.M. for an expedition into Finland. Soon after eleven we reached the frontier ; the road so far was badly paved and execrable, and where this was not the case there was no road at all, but deep sand. The moment we crossed into Finland the change was most remarkable, and the roads, though hilly, were very good. We stopped at Pampela, the second station in Finland, where we lunched at a clean post house upon provisions we had brought with us, for one could get little besides milk and eggs. The post houses generally were very small, and would have afforded but bad accommodation. The rope harness was very primitive, the horses were small but active, and the drivers looked very wild, but drove a tremendous pace. The road was hilly, and the speed with which we descended the hills fortunately carried us up them with a swing, as otherwise the little horses, which looked almost like cats harnessed to our heavy chariot, would inevitably have jibbed. The country was wooded, but monotonous, as the vegetation is almost entirely birch and fir, but after the flat roads in Russia the mere undulation was agreeable.

The first view of Viborg, which we reached a little past seven P.M., struck me as picturesque. The sun was setting behind the towers of the old town, and the hill from which we looked down upon it was covered, like the rest of Finland, with huge boulder stones. An inlet from the gulf of Finland runs up past Viborg. The fortifications erected by the Swedes were much as they were when the Russians took the place, except that the moats were dry, and the place looked neglected, though Viborg is a garrison town. There was a curious picturesque old tower, formerly a fort, now a prison. We drove through the town to Baron Nicolay's place, 'Mon Repos,' situated about one mile and a half from the town. Our host was for thirty years Russian Minister at Copenhagen, and had only lately retired from the Diplomatic Service to end his days at 'Mon Repos.' The house was clean and comfortable, and the garden well kept. The grounds were prettily undulated and rocky, bounded on one side by the sea. Baron

Nicolay was very fond of England and everything English, and piqued himself upon keeping his place 'à l'Anglaise.' He was a widower, and had three sons and three daughters. We spent Friday quietly at 'Mon Repos,' and started Saturday morning at six A.M. for the falls of Imatra, sixty versts off. The road was very hilly, but good, and we reached Imatra a little after eleven A.M. There we found a sort of pavilion erected for the accommodation of travellers, just over the falls, where we rested and dined. The two small inns looked very dirty and bad, and I should have been sorry to lodge in either of them. The rapids are fine, and the banks wooded. We went on to Sitola to see the upper fall, crossed the river Voxa and drove in *telegas* (little carts) to see the lake Saima, where the Voxa takes its source.

The view was very wild, the ground covered with rocks and heather, which was more agreeable to our sight than it was to our limbs, for the Finn boys who drove the little carts, which had no springs, were so proud of having us in lieu of a bundle of hay, that they insisted upon driving us full gallop across country, up hill and down dale, and as we could not make ourselves understood, there was nothing for it but to hold on like grim death, and be shaken to pieces. After spending a very pleasant day, we returned to 'Mon Repos' in the evening and spent Sunday there quietly. M. Kotin, the Governor of Viborg, came to dinner, and told me he was much interested in watching a plan of his, by which convicts were employed making a canal to unite the river Voxa to the sea. The men were not watched, and were under no restraint, only worked upon morally, and so far the plan had succeeded. They were well fed, and regularly paid for their labour. He told me, also, a curious anecdote of an event which happened about three weeks previously, in the parish of Kemlin, where there were a great number of wolves. A girl was working in the fields, when she was attacked by one of those ferocious creatures, which first bit her arm, and then leapt upon her back, with its paws on her shoulders. The girl, with great courage and presence of mind, put her hand into the animal's mouth and seized its tongue, which she held firmly till her cries brought assistance, and she was released from her perilous position, and the animal was killed. This fact was officially announced to M. Kotin, and reported by him to the Emperor. To give an idea of the primitive way in which horses are harnessed in Finland, I may mention that the harness is so made as to slip on and off at once. During our drive I heard a strange noise, and on looking out of the carriage I saw the harness of the off horse (we were driving four abreast) trailing on the ground, but the horse was cantering quietly along, as if nothing had happened.

Monday, September 30, 1847.—We left our pretty Villa Strogonoff, in the islands, where we had passed a very pleasant summer. The house was cheerful and comfortable, and my little garden so gay and full of flowers it was the astonishment of all beholders, and proved what could be done with a little care and trouble, for there were no flowers belonging to the place, so I planted all we had. We started at nine o'clock for Moscow, dined at 'Pomeranie,' drank tea at 'Sparskaia Polish,' travelled all night, breakfasted at Jagelbitze, and reached 'Vidropoursk,' where, as we found the post house tolerably clean, we halted, as I was very tired. We travelled in a chariot, and a fourgon followed with my maid and camp bed, which was a very necessary luxury, as most of the post houses are infested with bugs. At ten A.M. we left 'Vidropoursk,' and soon after met the Grand Duchess Marie and her husband returning to St. Petersburg at full gallop, which is the only way one ever wishes to travel in Russia, the roads are so uninteresting and the country so flat and ugly. Four horses were harnessed abreast, the driver generally stood up, his long hair streaming in the breeze, and he kept constantly hallooing to the horses, which all appeared to be going in different directions. The harness and carriage generally break once, if not twice, every stage, but people are so used to such accidents that they soon repair them, and one starts off again at full gallop.

Tver, where we dined on Wednesday, is the only picturesque town between Petersburg and Moscow. It is situated on the Volga, and looks Eastern; contains several large churches and convents, with domed roofs and high belfrys. Torjok (famous for its embroidered leather) is also a considerable place, but otherwise we saw nothing but long straggling villages, and often travelled miles and miles without seeing a human habitation of any sort or kind. We had thought of resting at Zavidowa, but found the place so dirty and uninviting, we pushed on to Moscow, which we reached on Thursday morning about 7.30 A.M. The first thing of interest one sees on approaching that town is the Palace of Petroffski, a large red and white building which was inhabited by Napoleon during his stay at Moscow. On the opposite side of the wood there was an immense plain, used as a race-course, and also for the military manœuvres. We saw the white tents of the soldiers in the distance, and to the right the domes, minarets, and towers of Moscow stretched far and wide. After driving through some uninteresting suburbs, we passed a boulevard and reached Howard's private hotel, which was clean and tolerably comfortable. Before leaving St. Petersburg we had heard uncomfortable reports that the cholera was travelling towards Moscow, and that there had been some cases there; but on our arrival we were told this was not true, though the terrible disease was undoubtedly approaching, and the Jean Tolstoys, who had just arrived from their estate at Varonesh, had lost their baby, maid, and nurse on the road. This was bad news, and made us rather anxious. However, having come so far, we determined to lionise the town, and we called on the governor and his wife, Prince and Princess Tcherbatoff, who received us with great courtesy and civility, and invited us to a ball the following Sunday, to meet the Grand Duke Michael. We then drove to the Kremlin, which is different from anything I had ever seen. Words fail me to describe its high battlemented walls, curious towers, and gilded domes, which are as unique as they are striking; and certainly the panoramic view of Moscow from the ramparts of the Kremlin is one of the finest sights in the world. The weather was very clear and bright, and I could hardly tear myself away from this wonderful view, but individually the churches disappointed me, as they are generally small.

We first visited the famous 'Vassili,' situated just outside the walls of the Kremlin. It is most curious and grotesque. The towers and domes are painted in bright colours, and the eye can with difficulty follow their outline. On the basement there is one small, dark, vaulted chapel, which contains the tomb of the saint, but on the first floor there is a perfect labyrinth of chapels and passages—one in the centre, and six others round it, connected by exterior and interior corridors.

The walls are immensely thick, and curiously painted in arabesque. The church was built in the reign of Ivan the Terrible, and it is said that after it was constructed he sent for the architect and expressed his approval of the building, asking at the same time, whether the architect thought he could build a still more elaborate church. He took a week to consider his answer; then his vanity got the better of his prudence, and he told the Czar he thought he *could* erect a still more curious church, upon which his eyes were put out, and he was imprisoned for life, the Czar declaring no one should have a finer church than himself. It certainly remains a standing memorial of the architect's ingenuity to satisfy the tyrant's caprice. Friday we went to see the five churches of the Kremlin, viz., the Assumption, the Annunciation, Archangel, St. Saviour's of the Miracles, and the Church of the Nunnery. The Assumption, or Cathedral, contains the tombs of the patriarchs, and is the church where the Emperors of Russia are crowned. It is very high, but dim and dingy, ill-kept, and we were particularly struck with the slovenly appearance of the priests, who were doing the service. The screen, which is said to be of real silver, is very high, and covered with icons, many of which were ornamented with large precious stones. Before the occupation of the town by the French the treasures of the various churches were all sent to the Troitzka monastery, about fifty versts from Moscow; and strange to say that place has never yet been taken, so the Russians consider it is under the immediate protection of Heaven, and miraculously preserved.

We saw the library and treasures of the Patriarchs—a curious collection of old plate, manuscripts, and some wonderful mitres and vestments richly embroidered in pearls. The service at the Church of the Nunnery is performed by the nuns;

the Abbess, surrounded by nuns, was reading aloud (the Psalms, I believe) in a gallery just above us, while below the nuns prostrated themselves before the different images; but I fear our presence disturbed their devotions, for they examined us with their eyes, and when we left they all ran to the church door to see us drive off. Friday being the day service is performed in the mosque, we drove to see the Mohammedans at their worship.

The building itself was wretched, in an out-of-the-way part of the town, not even plastered inside, and looked most dilapidated. The first thing we saw when we entered was a collection of dirty shoes, which the worshippers take off before entering the sacred precincts of the mosque. About thirty Asiatics, in their turbans and caftans, were present; they were either sitting in silence cross-legged on their carpets, or prostrating themselves and touching the ground with their foreheads. Before the conclusion of the service one of the men, dressed like the rest, but who we presumed was a Mufti, took the lead, and uttered a monotonous chant; after which he shut his eyes and spread out his hands, when all the others did the like. They remained in that attitude for a minute or two, then covered their faces with their hands, as if uttering a prayer; then the ceremony concluded, and they took their shoes and departed. I believe this is the only mosque a woman is allowed to enter. From thence we visited the Library of the Patriarchs, opposite the Church of the Assumption. We mounted a considerable flight of stairs, passed through several vaulted passages, and at length reached a small door guarded by a sentinel, when we met an old priest, who showed us the treasures. The first room contained a collection of ancient copes and vestments, some of which were very magnificent indeed, made of cloth of gold embroidered with real pearls. These were presents given by the Czars to the patriarchs, and some were as old as the reign of Ivan the Terrible, who was a contemporary of Queen Elizabeth. In the second room we found a large collection of curious old plate and the silver vessels which contain the holy oil, which is made at Moscow every three years, and then sent to various churches in Russia; there was also a collection of watches, chains, crosses, and relics which had belonged to the patriarchs. Beyond this room there was a small oratory, which was only remarkable as containing a curious vase in mother of pearl, which had been sent from Jerusalem, and was said to be copied from one used by Mary Magdalene!

On Saturday, Baron Bode, the Chamberlain, conducted us over the new Imperial Palace, which is very large and handsome. We first saw the throne room, then the staircase, order-room, and lastly, St. George's Hall, which was not completed, but which is two hundred and ten feet long, seventy wide, and proportionately high—a very splendid apartment. We were particularly struck by the beauty of the doors, made of Caucasian wood, which takes a high polish, and is beautifully veined and very ornamental. The kitchens in this new palace were very well arranged, and very large. On leaving the new palace we entered the old one, formerly the residence of the Czars, which is by far the most curious and interesting part of the Kremlin. The architecture is something between Venetian and Moresque, Italian architects having been employed by the Czar. The staircase, in painted stone, was picturesque and curious. The rooms were small, but also richly painted and gilt. The Czarewna's rooms, which consisted of two for herself and children, were immediately over the Czar's ; and the staircase leading to them was exceedingly narrow, and formerly was open to the outer air, which, as the cold in winter is intense at Moscow, does not agree with our notions of comfort and convenience. Peter the Great's father was the last Czar who lived in these apartments; his bed and furniture are still there, also his Psalter, which was curiously illuminated. The window of the Czar's room was distinguishable externally by its having a small column on either side, and petitioners had a right to enter the inner court of the palace, in order that they might be seen by the Czar, who then sent for their petitions. There are no less than seven small chapels in the old palace, most of them low and very dark, but richly gilt and decorated. One of them is curious from adjoining a room divided from it by arches, where the Czarewnas (who were not allowed by the Greek Church to enter a church ere forty days had elapsed after their confinement) were brought before childbirth, in order that they might take part in the services of the church, without being actually within the sacred precincts. In one of the very ancient chapels some workmen were employed, when they found that the wall sounded hollow; and on breaking through the wall a niche was discovered which, it is said, was inhabited for many years by a recluse. It is much too small to allow even a very small man to stand up or lie down in any comfort, so it must have been a painful abode. On leaving the palace we went to a large ugly building erected by the Emperor Alexander, where the Crown treasures were deposited. The first room was filled with armour, flags, and trophies of different kinds, and lying neglected and dusty in one corner was the Constitution of Poland, shut up in an old velvet case. Fit emblem of the decadence of that once prosperous and powerful kingdom, which was civilised and flourishing when Russia was uncivilised and barbarous. In the second room there was a fine collection of old plate, and a case containing several relics of Peter the Great. The third room contained many crowns of different shapes, sizes, and countries, the thrones of the various Czars, and a vast quantity of jewels. The precious stones are, however, badly cut, and are therefore less striking than they ought to be, but there is a wonderful profusion of them; the crowns and several of the thrones were richly inlaid with them. The Coronation robes were many of them embroidered with pearls. In another room, filled with arms of different sizes and dates, we saw Napoleon's camp bed taken during the retreat from Moscow in 1812–13. It was a small soft downy couch, and in a pocket of the pillow-case the Emperor kept his private papers. M. Kakoschkine—a clever, agreeable man

—did the honours of this part of the Kremlin, and showed us the most remarkable things; but the collection was much too large to be seen in detail in one day. Among other curiosities there was a number of old carriages, which had belonged to the patriarchs and Czars. One had been painted by Watteau, and another little vehicle belonged to Peter the Great as a child.

We visited the Simonoff convent at the outskirts of the town—a large and curious building, from which there is a fine view of Moscow. The chanting in that church was peculiar, but I thought it very monotonous and uninteresting. The Archimandrite who was present was a fine old man, with a long grey beard and benign expression of countenance. The black flowing dress of the monks and their high caps were striking and picturesque. On leaving the Simonoff convent we visited St. Sauveur's. Service was going on, and the church was quite full, so I declined pressing through the crowd—never a pleasant operation, but particularly odious when it is composed of Russians in their filthy sheepskins; and woe to the unhappy wight who comes in contact with the peasants in Russia! As it was, I generally returned from my trips richer than when I left home; though I was fortunate in escaping all vermin, except the light cavalry, which tormented me dreadfully.

Sunday, September 27.—We attended divine service in the English chapel, where we found a large and very respectable congregation. Immediately after church we drove up to the Sparrow Hills to see the departure of the prisoners for Siberia, who are sent off every Sunday between one and two o'clock. The prison was a wretched place, merely a collection of small wooden houses which had been erected in the time of the cholera in 1831, in order that the prisoners, who come from all parts of the country, should not be brought into the infected town. We first entered a room where the prisoners were being examined by Dr. Haas. That excellent man had devoted himself to them for seventeen years, and had obtained great influence over them and the authorities. He talked and reasoned with them, listened to their various tales and complaints, tried to lead them to repentance and dependence on their Saviour. Before starting every prisoner received a present of money, clothes, and books. The sight of so many fellow creatures doomed, in consequence of fearful crimes, to spend the rest of their days in hardship and suffering, was a very sad one, and impressed me deeply. Two texts of

Scripture came into my mind, viz., 'To whom much is given, of him shall much be required,' and 'Many that are first shall be last, and the last shall be first;' and I felt as if I had never realised them as fully as I did at that moment.

There were in all about eighty prisoners—men, women, and children; twenty-eight were going to the mines for life, having committed dreadful murders. The other prisoners were going to the different governments and stations in Siberia, exiled for life, but able, if they behaved well, to earn a tolerable and respectable livelihood. They were all warmly clad, with good new shoes, and looked fairly clean. The men had one side of their heads, beards, and eyebrows shaved clean off, which gave them a most ghastly appearance; but this is done in order that they may be recognised in case they escape during the march.

A few had fearful countenances, but generally they looked more apathetic and stupid than either wicked or unhappy. When I entered the prison one wretched convict was on his knees at Haas' feet, in an attitude of the humblest but most earnest supplication, and sobbing as if his heart would break. His history was curious. He was sent to Siberia for murder, and his wife declined accompanying him thither, which wives have always the option of doing if they please; but in case they refuse the marriage is considered annulled, and the woman is at liberty to marry again. In the present case this convict had contrived to escape, and had walked back to his village in White Russia, living upon roots, hiding by day, and walking by night. When he reached his home he found his wife had married another man; he was again taken prisoner, and when I saw him, was being sent back to Tobolsk, to take his trial as a renegade; but he was earnestly begging to be allowed to take his wife back with him. In vain he was told that this was out of the question, he would not be tranquillised, until, at length, after having exhausted all his powers of persuasion, Dr. Haas referred him to a priest, who told him he must endeavour to resign himself to God's will, who saw fit to deny the wish of his heart in order to lead him to repentance, and wean his affections from all earthly blessings, that he might fix them more entirely upon heaven and heavenly things. The poor wretch listened with attention and apparent thankfulness, but despair and misery were written on his countenance, and he looked the picture of guilt and sorrow, and went away weeping bitterly.

I next saw a Jew and his wife and children. The two former were accused of being the accomplices of a servant who had murdered his master, but they were going *en famille* to the colonies, and looked thoroughly contented and jolly! The last thing he tried was to get some money from Dr. Haas, to pay a small tax levied on the Jews, to make up a sum which one of them had robbed and carried off. He was delighted when we gave him the small sum of twenty kopecks. Dr. Haas next led me up to another Jew, with whom he reasoned, asking him how he could conceive that the Messiah had *not* come, when the prophecies concerning Him have been accomplished, and the sceptre has departed from Judah. The man looked rather puzzled, but immediately said, 'Oh, that's all very well, and what you Gentiles tell us, but our Rabbis teach us very differently, and I do not believe the sceptre *has* departed from Judah.' Haas, rather taken aback at this assertion, said, 'Well, but you know Jerusalem was destroyed by the Romans, and there has been no king since.' 'Oh,' said the man, 'there *is* a king somewhere,' pointing to the East, 'I do not know exactly where; but somewhere in India.'

Before the prisoners started they were all

placed in a row and their names called over, then all the Christians turned their faces towards the Church and crossed themselves, one or two of them prostrating themselves, and touching the ground with their foreheads after the manner of the Greeks. They then approached Haas, kissed his hands and the hem of his garment, blessed and thanked him for all his goodness and kindness towards them. He took leave of each individually, giving a few words of consolation and advice, and when they were off he turned to me and said very solemnly that his prayer always was, not only for himself, but for all the authorities, that at the great day of judgment when all met again in the presence of God, they might not in their turn be accused by the very men who were undergoing the severest punishment for their crimes.

A hospital was attached to the prison under Dr. Haas' superintendence, who was himself a medical man, and never allowed the prisoners to start if they were sick or in an unfit condition to undertake the journey, which lasts five months and a half. They walk about twenty miles a day, and rest every third day. They are allowed carts to carry their luggage, women, and children ; and when they start their clothes are in good order, but I believe they undergo dreadful hardships on the march, from cold, fatigue, and ill-treatment, though Dr. Haas assured me that very few die on the way. The sight was curious, interesting, and impressive, but extremely sad.

The view of Moscow from the Sparrow Hills is very grand indeed. The river winds below, the town spreads far beyond with its gilt domes and towers. On returning we stopped to see the Empress's Villa Alexandria, which was not remarkable, and there was such a pestilential smell there from the sewers, which were just outside the barrier, and a very short distance from the Palace, that I was glad to get away from it. The Domskoi convent is the most celebrated in the environs of Moscow. It is surrounded by a very curious brick wall with battlements and towers, and the church is very large and fine; but to my mind all Greek churches are more or less alike, and the profusion of gilt images in them may give them a rich appearance, but at the same time a very barbarous one, and I remembered with pleasure the simple grandeur of our fine Gothic cathedrals, so much more conducive, I imagine, to devotional feeling than the glitter and bad taste of a Greek church.

Monday, September 28. — We visited the wonderful Foundling Hospital, which we were told contained the day we were there 7,000 souls! We first went through the establishment for the education of young girls, chiefly officers' daughters. The different classes seemed arranged with great care, and those who wish to learn may there have a very good education. They are taught French and German, drawing, music, geography, arithmetic, and various kinds of needlework. They are educated to be governesses, and at the age of eighteen or nineteen are sent out of the school. They are clothed, fed, and educated solely at the expense of the Crown, and when they leave the establishment each receives a small sum of money. During six years after leaving, should they lose their situations or their health, they have a right to return as to a home, and are well taken care of. I heard several of the girls play the pianoforte, which they certainly did very well; but the lady at the head of the establishment, who took us over it, told me that when any girl shows a decided talent for any particular branch of education, it is always cultivated, and therefore the young ladies I heard play were among those in the school who showed the greatest talent for music. There were then 700 pupils in the establishment, and we saw their dormitory and dinners. The upper story of the house was given up to the Foundlings, and is quite apart from the school. When a baby is left at the door of the hospital, it is washed and christened, unless a small cross is found hung round its neck in token that it has already been baptised. It is then given a wet nurse, and kept a month at the hospital to ascertain that it is in good health, after which the nurse takes it away to her village, and keeps it to the age of fourteen, receiving a silver rouble (*3s. 2d.*) a week for its keep. It must then work for its livelihood; but all children left at the Foundling Hospital were free, which was considered a great privilege. The numbers dependent upon the hospital were immense, and amounted, we were informed, to 30,000. The nurses were all dressed alike in the Russian costume, and it was a pretty sight to see them ranged in line as we passed through the rooms; but the atmosphere was anything but agreeable, and I was glad to get away from it; in winter, when the house is shut up, it must be dreadful.

We passed an ancient gateway, called 'La porte rouge,' which was picturesque; and an old tower, called 'La tour de sucre,' now used as a reservoir to supply the fountains in Moscow, was very fine.

We went to a pleasant small party at

Princess Lwoff's in the evening, and Tuesday started at twelve o'clock for General Boutourlines' place, Troitska, fourteen versts from Moscow. The first half of the way was on the *chaussée,* but the latter half gave me a specimen of Russian roads, and certainly all I had heard of their atrocity had given me but a faint notion of the reality. Deep sand, always uneven, and sometimes full of immense holes, threatened to break the carriage at every step. Occasionally, in a village trees were laid down by way of improvement, which used to be called corderoy roads, but as these very soon decay, they make the road worse than it was before. However, more by good luck than good management, we arrived safely, and found a nice country house overlooking the Moskwa, and close to a very fine church, which was built by Peter the Great's mother. It was much better painted than one usually sees, and the architecture was very pretty. After luncheon the Boutourlines' drove us to Archangliska, a magnificent place belonging to Prince Yousoupoff. It was in bad repair, but a very large house, with a stone colonnade, and the rooms immensely large. The best pictures had been removed to St. Petersburg, but there were two pyramidal sideboards covered with very fine old china. The garden was in the French style, with groves of straight cut lime-trees, and a large collection of marble busts and statues. The orangery was immense, and contained some of the finest orange-trees I ever saw. There was also a curious collection of old state carriages, like those at the Kremlin, which had been used at different coronations.

Mints of money must have been laid out at Archangliska, which nevertheless looked neglected and forlorn. It seems, Prince Yousoupoff, in spite of having such a magnificent place, was not famous for his liberality. He gave a *fête* to the Emperor Alexander during the King of Prussia's visit to Moscow, which everyone expected would be very splendid, instead of which there was a simple cold collation ; after which he proposed his guests should go to his theatre, which was in the garden. There they found half a dozen musicians in the orchestra, and whilst these performed some indifferent music, the curtain lifted and displayed a scene, but no actors ; this was repeated several times, till all the scenes had been shown, when the entertainment was said to be finished, and the guests returned to Moscow grumbling at the shabby reception they had met with ! We went back to

Troitska for dinner, and then took our leave of our kind hosts, as I did not like the idea of travelling over such a perilous road in the dark. Wednesday, we visited Melnitze, Prince Galitzin's place, fourteen versts across an uninteresting sandy plain. The house was not large, but the grounds were extensive and beautifully kept; from Melnitze we drove to Kuskowa, Count Schérémétieff's. Also a large place with a French garden and quantities of statues and orange-trees. There was a large and curious collection of portraits, and a grotto made of shells with figures of the same, more singular than artistic. We left Moscow on Friday morning on our return to St. Petersburg; the weather was very sultry and hot, and as I was very tired, we stopped to sleep at Mednoja. The next morning we felt a great change in the atmosphere, and rain fell Saturday and Saturday night. On reaching Novgorod Sunday morning, we found the post-house so filthy, we were glad to get out of it as quickly as possible. The cold there was intense, and a bitter wind was blowing; we, however, determined to see a famous convent in the neighbourhood, which is one of the richest in Russia, having been endowed by a certain Countess Orloff in memory of her father, to redeem his soul from purgatory. The road was very rough, and on arriving we found service going on in the principal church, where the jewels are kept, so we could not examine them minutely, but they are very fine; and one cross, in an icon of John the Baptist, was made of five large diamonds. Countess Orloff was Abbess of the convent, and lived there many years. She died quite suddenly at the altar when she was in the act of receiving the Holy Communion. A very blessed ending to a holy life devoted to charity and prayer. The altar was in silver, the music was good, the priests' vestments very fine, and altogether the service was better done than in any other church I had visited. The convent itself is very large, and there were three churches within its precincts.

Whilst we were drinking tea that evening at Pomerania, a vehicle arrived with snow on the roof, and our dismay was great when, shortly after we had started, a violent snowstorm began. I never was out in such a fearful night. The wind howled and the snow fell so heavily, that it was soon up to the axle-trees of the carriages, and obliterated all traces of the road. All the post-houses were closed, so that there was much delay in getting horses; and instead of reaching home comfortably at bed-time, we thought ourselves very fortunate in arriving, without serious accident, the following morning at 5 A.M., dead tired with our long and weary journey, but very thankful to be once more in our own clean and comfortable house, Dom Strukoff, on the English quay.

CHAPTER XI.

The Grand Duke Constantine took the Oath of Allegiance—The Cholera—I return to England—Letter from Lord Bloomfield—Letter from General Baron L——A portrait of General Lamoricière—Visits to Welikina and Narva—Death of Sir Robert Peel—Russian Superstitions—Ball at the Winter Palace—A Story of Cracow—We leave St. Petersburg and visit Warsaw.

December 8, 1847.—The Corps Diplomatique were invited to assist at the ceremony of the Grand Duke Constantine taking the oath of allegiance to his father, elder brothers, and his heirs, according to the rule established by the Emperor Nicholas: each Grand Duke, on coming of age, is obliged to take the oath of allegiance in order to avoid all doubt as to the succession. On our arrival at the Winter Palace we were conducted to the Chapel. The Imperial family had already taken their places within the altar rails. After a short service, performed by the Metropolitan and his attendant priests, who wore splendid vestments, there was some beautiful music, and then the Emperor led the Grand Duke

Constantine up to the altar, and after making the sign of the cross and kissing the Bible, the latter read the oath in a clear voice, and with his hand upraised. He seemed very much impressed, and, as soon as he had read the oath, he was blessed and embraced by his father and mother, who were both much affected. He then embraced his brothers and sisters, and his betrothed, the young Princess Alexandrine of Saxe-Altenburg, who stood immediately in front of me. She was tall and had a fine figure; the upper part of her face was exceedingly handsome. It was a curious coincidence that she was said to resemble the late Grand Duchess Alexandrine so much, that when first the Empress saw her on her arrival Her Majesty burst into tears, exclaiming, 'Oh, Aline, ma chère, chère enfant.' After the service in the chapel, we all went to St. George's Hall, which was full of soldiers, and we took up our places immediately on the right of the throne. The room was very large and handsome, and opposite the throne was a small altar, and the Emperor's confessor, in full canonicals, stood by it. A flourish of trumpets announced the approach of the Imperial family, followed by the officers of state and court. The Emperor led the Empress up to the throne, the Hereditary Grand Duchess stood to the right, the other Grand Duchesses and the Princess of Altenburg to the left, the Czar himself stood next his son near the altar, and again the Grand Duke Constantine repeated the oath of allegiance after the confessor. As soon as it was ended, the Emperor turned to the troops, and, as head of the army, gave the word of command, upon which they presented arms. This act was so characteristic of the Emperor that every one was struck by it. It completed the ceremony, which was one of the most impressive and interesting I ever witnessed.

In the spring of 1848, revolutions broke out all over Europe. Count de Rayneval was at that time Chargé d'Affaires of France at St. Petersburg, and one day my husband was paying him a visit, when suddenly the secretary walked into the room, and to his intense dismay and astonishment, addressed him with the words—'Citoyen de France, la République est déclarée.' Poor M. de Rayneval nearly fell backwards, he was so taken by surprise; but sure enough we soon after heard that Louis Philippe had fled, and Paris was in arms.

The cholera which, as I have already stated, had shown itself in the south of Russia in 1847, ceased during the winter; but every one said it would break out again in the spring, and advance, as it had done previously, about 30 versts a day!

Sure enough, early in the spring, we heard of it at Moscow, then at Twer, Novgorod, and at last a few cases appeared at St. Petersburg. Then it rapidly increased, and the whole city was plague-stricken. The air was excessively sultry and oppressive. The doctors ordered the people not to fast; but they would sooner have died than obey this injunction; and when the cholera was at its height, and as many as eleven hundred people dying a day, the churches were full of open coffins, as it is usual to bless the bodies and sprinkle them with holy water before interment.

We moved out to the Nicholl's Datcha in the island, and soon after that, as I was very much out of health, the doctors ordered me to quit St. Petersburg. I went down to Peterhof to take leave of the Emperor and Empress, and in order to do so, had to drive through the town and past the cholera hospital. As we approached it, I saw a poor man driving up in a droschky, supported by another man, and as he passed close by my side of the carriage, I saw that his jaw had dropped; he was quite blue, and looked ghastly. I own I was much alarmed and greatly shocked. I felt as if an electric current had passed through me, and I turned icy cold; but I said nothing to my husband, who was sitting by my side. As soon as I got to Peterhof, I asked for some sherry, and drank off a glass, which restored animation, and I got through my audience, and was none the worse for the fright. Two days after I departed for England. Two boats were leaving, one for Lubeck, the other, twenty-four hours later, for Stettin, and I begged hard to be allowed to take the shorter passage; but my husband, who was anxious I should get off, decided I had better leave by the Lubeck boat, which I did, and, thank God, had a prosperous and fine passage.

No less than three people died on board the boat, which sailed the next day for Stettin, and had this occurred whilst I was on board, the consequences might have been serious. Of course my husband had to send in to town every day for his letters; but he only went in once a week himself to despatch the messengers. One day our *chasseur* begged to be allowed to fetch the post instead of the Chancery servant, as he wished to see some friends. On arriving at their house, he saw nine coffins carried out one after the other, and this gave him such a shock, he returned home, and was seized soon after; but the doctor, who was sent for immediately, declared it was more fright than cholera, and after a few hours of bed and a dose of brandy the man was all right. Except this false alarm our household mercifully escaped, which my husband attributed, in some measure, to the strong rice-soup with which he fed his servants. One very terrible catastrophe happened. Twenty young students, who had passed their examination satisfactorily, determined to celebrate the event by a dinner. Whether they drank more champagne than was good for them or not I know not, but the following day out of twenty eighteen were dead; and our friends, the Bobrinsky's, who lived near us in the Islands, had no less than seventeen cases of cholera in their house.

The question of drainage was very little understood when I was at St. Petersburg, and nothing could well be worse than it was then. The odours in the spring were most offensive, and the Neva water was very deleterious, so that no one could drink it with impunity.

Letters from my Husband during the Visitation of the Cholera at St. Petersburg.

St. Petersburg, July 3, 1848.—There was a little disturbance in town on Saturday, and it was found necessary to punish the ringleaders of the mob which got up the poisoning row. Some were publicly flogged at Vassili Ostroff, and the Emperor Nicholas made his appearance in the middle of the punishment and ordered it to be stopped; but spoke to the people in the firm manner which he recommends to others; told them that these rows were a disgrace to Russia; but that as long as he was alive they should never have any serious consequences. He then addressed the soldiers who were drawn up near the scene of punishment, told them he knew he could always count upon them; they answered by a cheer, and the mob dispersed after having obtained of the Emperor the promise of a Greek Church procession. This came off yesterday, and the streets were crowded with people, but no disorder took place. All this proves the unbounded influence possessed by the Emperor over his people, their confidence in him, and the tact with which he can always manage them. However, the procession has had one very unfortunate effect; this bringing the masses together has greatly increased the number of cases of cholera. I am taking every human precaution against the disease. Hitherto God has been very merciful to me and my house, and I pray for a continuance of His protecting hand over all belonging to us.

July 17.—I have just been perusing a paper which Count Nesselrode has sent me, which makes us both hope that an armistice has really been signed between the Germans and Danes. I shall rejoice most sincerely at this event, as an armistice once signed, we may confidently hope that peace will naturally follow. Indeed, I believe both parties would gladly get out of this business, and that but for those gentlemen at Frankfort, the affair would have been settled long since.

July 6.—Poor S—— is no more. He has been suffering from a tendency to paralysis for years past; he was seized with the prevailing epidemic, and died almost without pain. I saw him a short time ago in my room in town, when he spoke to me under great apprehensions of cholera; his last words were: 'God knows if we shall ever meet again—watch and be careful.' This is one of the victims of the system of passports in this country; the poor man has been applying for six months past for permission to go abroad for his health; he would have gone at the opening of the navigation if his passport had been granted, and here is the result!

I went into town yesterday for the first time since you left, and it is a dismal affair: one meets nothing but coffins, people in mourning, and an anxious look on the countenance of every person. The air in the town (the day was hot) was dreadfully oppressive, and I felt I breathed much more comfortably in the Islands. I had a visit from General Berg—he has 2,000 people living in the 'État Major,' but he says he has established a system of police and cleanliness which has succeeded admirably so far, for he has had but one case of cholera under his roof. I met Doctor Mianoffsky at the Strogonoffs, a Pole, who has performed wonders in his hospital by the use of laudanum to a vast extent. He told me he certainly considers the disease to be less intense, though the cases perhaps are still on the increase. Dr. Wrangel paid me a visit this morning. He never leaves the Islands night or day, so one has a chance of getting him if wanted, a better one at least than if he attended some town hospital, which almost all the doctors do. The poor man looked fearfully worked, and told me he had not been in bed for four nights, that all he could find time to do was to dress and wash himself, that sleep was out of the question. I cannot think that the disease is contagious, because out of the 800 doctors in St. Petersburg, only one has taken the cholera. He died.

July 13.—I saw Mianoffsky, just returned from a trip to Peterhof; he seemed more dead than alive; but he comforted us by the assurance that there is every appearance of the cholera being on the decline, as fewer new cases have been brought into the hospital, and there were actually unoccupied beds! so that if the disease decreases in the present ratio, we may expect that the epidemic will cease altogether in about three weeks! I do not believe all this, but it was consoling to our spirits. The S—— house is dreadful in one respect, for they really talk and think of nothing else, and work themselves into a state of nervousness which is painful to behold, and must tend to bring on the disease. All the Corps Diplomatique have taken up their quarters in the Islands, and there is not a creature in St. Petersburg that can possibly be away from it. This is satisfactory, as one may hope the disease will thus have less spread, and cease the sooner. However, it is sad enough to know that it has reappeared, and with great violence too, in almost all the towns in Russia which it visited last year. This is a melancholy fact, as it makes one fear that cholera will take root in this country, and if it does so in Russia, it may possibly do so in the rest of Europe, or at all events in those parts where the population live upon food calculated to produce and keep up the disease.

August 1, 1848.—The sanitary condition of the metropolis is improving, but the apple season is coming on, and people are horridly afraid that when this fruit is blessed by the bishops (which is a sort of religious ceremony in this country, and about to take place), that the lower orders will devour them with avidity, and produce a return of the disease. It is now very bad at Riga, and about 160,000 people have died of cholera in Russia from its appearance last autumn to the 1st of July!

Lord Bloomfield joined me in England in October, and the following year went to meet the Queen on Her Majesty's first visit to Ireland.

Exracts of Letters from my Husband.

Palmerston House, August 7, 1849.—Little did I think when I was writing to you last night from the cabin of the 'Cambria,' that the rain was so soon to come down in torrents. It began as soon as we made the lights, and poured incessantly the whole night, so my landing was not particularly pleasant. When we got to Dublin station there was not a car to be seen, or any conveyance ; but after a little patience, and the services of an intelligent little boy, I got a car, and in the midst of a deluge started for Palmerston, which I was told was five miles off, instead of three, as I had calculated. How you would have laughed to see my start from Dublin, bringing a ragged boy to hold the trunks together, as we had no ropes to fasten them, and then the driver did not know the place well. We picked up another boy to show us the gate, but arrived safe at last about 1 A.M. ! Fortunately the weather was lovely for the Queen's landing, and everything went off well. Dublin and Kingstown were brilliantly illuminated, and as the rain did not begin till ten o'clock, the public had enough of it.

Palmerston, August 8.—I am just come back from the Review, which was perfection. The Queen was immensely cheered, and there must have been at least 150,000 people out! Her Majesty seemed greatly pleased ; the weather charming, no rain or dust, but very sultry. Last night I was at the Phœnix Park till nearly twelve. There was some Irish music, but the society did not seem very lively. Lord Clarendon seems greatly pleased about the Queen's reception, and told me that Her Majesty's visit to Dublin with

Lady Clarendon yesterday, without any body or escort, was a famous *coup d'état*! I must say that I never saw such good feeling, or apparent attachment to the Sovereign, displayed in any country. It was very pleasant to see, and the more so as it was quite spontaneous, and certainly not got up by drink or anything of the kind. I hear the landing at Kingstown was a most beautiful sight, the enthusiasm of the people, and the cheering deafening.

Old Mrs. George Villiers is here, and her motherly feelings have been much gratified by the success which has attended all the arrangements for Her Majesty's reception, and she thinks it is Lord Clarendon's triumph, as it seems that he it was who first proposed the journey.

Lady Londonderry (Frances Anne) has got the first floor at Morrisson's, and drives about in her fine coach and grey horses. She brought over her washing and other things, all in silver, to the astonishment of poor Paddy, who is unaccustomed to such luxuries! The Prince had a little Review this morning, and the artillery were banging away at half-past eight. The day is dreadfully close and disagreeable, and as there will be a fearful crush at the levée, I do not know what will become of us all.

We returned to Russia in October 1849, and remained there till we quitted St. Petersburg in 1851 for Berlin.

Copy of a Letter from General Baron L——.

St.-Pétersbourg, Octobre 1849.—Vous me demandez si je connais, si je vois le général Lamoricière ? Je vous répondrai affirmativement oui, je le vois, je le connais, je lui parle et il fait semblant de m'écouter, mais le plus souvent c'est lui qui parle et je l'écoute avec plaisir, car il s'énonce bien, raisonne admirablement et même logiquement. Il sait beaucoup de choses et sans être pédant et boutonné, comme le sont souvent les diplomates, il se laisse entraîner par la matière, et dit alors plus que ces messieurs se permettroient d'avouer.

Il est petit de taille, ramassé, porte des moustaches énormes et une impériale monstreuse, a un regard très-fin, sans cependant être faux, est très-aimable et très-spirituel avec les femmes, qui prennent promptement goût pour lui. Il me rappelle parfois les héros des romans de Paul de Kock, dont la tournure se ressent toujours un peu de l'estaminet, sans dégénérer en rudesse ou en ridicule : enfin on s'aperçoit promptement qu'il n'est pas un enfant du Faubourg St. Germain ou de la Chaussée d'Antin, mais un élève de St. Cyr ou de l'Ecole polytechnique, qui a la conviction qu'il sait quelque chose de mieux que de tirer la révérence en trois temps.

J'avois laissé écouler sans m'y frotter la première Mission Républicaine. La couleur rouge m'est odieuse, et je ne la tolère que sur les parements de nos uniformes. Je m'imaginois que la mission du général Lamoricière auroit le même sort ! mais il n'en fut pas ainsi.

A un grand diner chez le Ministre des Domaines l'obligéant comte de Kisseleff nous rapprocha : je lachois au général français alors des complimens à bout portant sur ses antécédents en Afrique, que d'ailleurs chaque coiffeur parisien auroit mieux tourné, mais auxquels tout Français, fut-il le sabreur le plus intrépide, sera toujours sensible. Après le diner, l'Amphitrion nous réunit dans son cabinet autour d'un bon feu et le sociable cigarre fut présenté. Alors mon intrépide preneur de barricades fondit, car il faut savoir que Lamoricière ne comprend pas la vie sociale sans ce narcotique ; mais une fois la carotte dans la bouche, il se trouva tout-à-fait à son aise et nous transporta promptement en Afrique, à Isly et à la soumission d'Abdel Kader. J'avois pris l'initiative pour le faire arriver à cette conversation intéressante pour nous tous, j'avois mis en mouvement les rouages de ma méthode, c'est à dire, de ne parler à des hommes de cette trempe que d'eux-mêmes, de ce qui les intéresse, et pas du tout de nous, de nos intérêts, de sorte qu'il se trouvait tout d'abord satisfait et à son aise, sa parole coulait de source, il étoit sur son champ de bataille, et alors il nous analysa avec une grande lucidité et beaucoup de franchise la composition et la portraiture du nouveau ministère qui vint de surgir de dessous terre ; il falloit être bien stupide pour ne pas y trouver un intérêt.

Ayant quitté cette séance après moi, il remercia le comte Kisseleff de lui avoir procuré l'avantage de faire la connaissance 'd'un vieux troupier.' Notez que je n'avois rien dit ou peu de choses, lui seul avoit parlé, je n'avois fait que de le traiter en cheval fringant, auquel il faut de temps à autre faire sentir le mors et le jarret pour le faire marcher d'un pas régulier. Mon mérite consistoit donc à le faire parler, ce qui pour les hommes doués d'une imagination vive sera toujours la corde qu'il faudra toucher pour leur rendre toute société agréable ; c'est un secret social que je vous confie, et il y a plus d'adresse là-dedans qu'on ne se l'imagine vulgairement. Que me fait à moi qu'il trouve nos bataillons superbes, nos escadrons magnifiques, nos institutions militaires admirables, nos hôpitaux dignes d'éloges? Je sais tout cela, mais je veux savoir ce qu'on fait chez eux; c'est à coup sûr plus instructif que les complimens qu'on nous adressera et que d'ailleurs nous savons très bien nous faire à nous-mêmes.

A présent le sobriquet de 'vieux troupier' m'est resté, je les avois toujours échappés, il falloit que le représentant du peuple de la Sarthe arrive pour m'en affubler. Depuis nous nous voyons souvent et il paroît que le sabreur moderne a pris du goût pour 'le vieux troupier' qui, bien entendu, il n'ose pas aborder de ce sobriquet, mais à qui il adresse volontiers celui de 'mon ancien' titre très-usité en langage militaire en France, lorsqu'on veut témoigner à un individu l'amitié et l'estime qu'on lui porte.

Vous voyez d'après ce que je viens de vous dire qu'il est loin d'être talon rouge, sans cependant être embarrassé de tourner une phrase très-agréablement et surtout toujours spirituellement. Ses phrases sont rondes, jamais sucrées, et c'est à tort qu'on lui en veut dans quelques-uns de nos salons, dans lesquels les gens superficiels ne veulent pas comprendre qu'un homme de notre époque extraordinaire ne peut pas ressembler aux marquis d'autrefois. Ses réponses sont toujours précises, brèves, franches ; il ne torture pas la parole pour masquer sa pensée ou son jugement. Il répondit, par exemple, à l'Impératrice qui lui avoit fait l'honneur de lui demander comment il avoit trouvé son beau régiment des chevaliers-gardes, lors de son entrée de la promenade en Pologne ? 'Madame, votre régiment est beau, magnifique, mais les chevaux avoient l'air de souffrir et d'avoir mal au ventre !' Son jugement étoit juste, l'Empereur avoit été peu satisfait de l'état dans lequel ce régiment lui fut présenté, mais on trouva, et je crois avec raison, que la réponse de Lamoricière sentoit un peu trop la caserne ou l'écurie.

Cette incongruité que l'on blâme beaucoup dans nos salons fut cependant réparée par le mot heureux qu'il eut l'honneur d'adresser à l'Empereur, qui lui demanda son opinion sur nos grenadiers en le prévenant qu'il s'attendoit bien à des complimens, mais qu'il ne les désiroit pas, y étant trop habitué. 'Sire,' lui répondit Lamoricière, 'avec des gaillards de cette espèce on fait de la bonne politique !'

Sa résolution est toujours prompte, instantanée : c'est un homme d'action ! L'autre jour à une revue, étant à la suite de l'Empereur, un cheval de lancier glissa sur le verglas et tombe. Tout le monde le voit, personne n'a la présence d'esprit de courir au secours. Lamoricière d'un bond de son cheval se précipite, relève le lancier et revint tranquillement se replacer à la suite de l'Empereur. Il repart ces jours-ci pour Paris. Le dernier mot de sa vie n'est pas encore dit, comme le boulet qui devoit toucher Napoléon n'a jamais été fondu. Son énergie, son courage, son éloquence de tribune le feront toujours compter pour quelque chose, et les circonstances qui l'entraînent le forceront de jouer un rôle. Je termine en concluant que je ne serois pas désireux de voir le blanc des yeux de cet homme vis-à-vis de moi métamorphosé en ennemi.

I knew General Lamoricière very well, and this description of him is true and characteristic. He was diffident and rather shy in ladies' society, and extremely sensitive. One evening when I was alone he came to pay me a visit, and found me occupied with my crochet, which I did not think it necessary to discontinue, as it in no way interfered with my giving my full attention to my guest. However, at the end of a very few minutes he took his hat to depart. I asked, rather surprised, whether he was going elsewhere, and why he was in such a hurry; so he assured me he had not disposed of his evening, but as I did not give him my undivided attention, he imagined I did not care for his society! On another occasion we met at a ball, and after looking at some pretty girls who were dancing, he turned round to me with a satirical smile, and said, 'Ah! madame, si vous saviez comme cela m'amuse de voir les femmes tricoter ainsi avec leurs jambes!'

He was such an inveterate smoker that at home he had a pipe or a cigar in different parts of the room. When my husband called upon him on business, he never sat down, but kept walking up and down the room, taking a puff first at one and then at the other.

Old General Löwenstern, the writer of the above letter, was one of the cleverest and most entertaining men at St. Petersburg; he had been in the army which followed the French in the retreat from Moscow, and he told me the whole road was strewn with the bodies of men and horses. The Russians were so hardened to this sight, that frequently when they halted for dinner or supper, instead of sitting down on the snow, the officers called out, 'Daï Franzuski' ('give me a Frenchman'), and they threw a cloak or horse-rug over the frozen corpse, and sat upon it. The hospitals were overcrowded, and pestilential. At one place the cold was so intense, that the broken windows had been blocked up with pieces of human flesh instead of glass!

We left the Forestier's, where we had spent the summer, on July 4, to pay Count and Countess Zavadoffsky a visit at Welikina, their nice place near Narva. The country there is prettier than anything I had seen in Russia. The ground was varied, wooded and very wild. The house was comfortable, and remarkably well furnished; it was situated opposite a deep ravine, and the view from the windows was charming. The grounds and garden were well laid out, and except from the roughness of the roads the drives in the neighbourhood would have been delightful. Several large lakes were within easy reach, and the Gulf of Finland was only ten versts off. We spent three very pleasant days at Welikina, but the weather at first was intensely hot, and the first night, as our room was immediately under the copper roof of the house and very low, I thought we should have been smothered. We were obliged to leave the windows open, the consequence being that we were devoured by mosquitoes, and when we rose in the morning our faces and hands looked as if we had the small-pox,

I had a French maid with me who amused herself killing these cruel insects whilst I was at breakfast, and when I came up to my room she said to me, 'Milady, voyez donc les cadavres,' and sure enough I counted ninety-three on the window-sill; but the following night we rested in peace.

The dress of the peasants at Welikina was exceedingly pretty and picturesque; they brought large plates full of wild strawberries for sale every day, which had the peculiar flavour and aroma of the Alpine strawberries, and were, I thought, very much better than the large fruit we have in England.

On Monday, July 8, we left our kind friends to visit Narva, where Baron Stieglitz, the owner of a large cloth manufactory, had kindly placed his apartment at our disposal. It was situated on the banks of the Narowa, about four versts from Narva, but close to the waterfalls, which were one of the objects of our visit. M. Pelzer showed us over the manufactory, which was very large, and employed about 800 persons. They worked thirteen hours a day, and only received three roubles and a half a month, about eleven shillings; one rouble and a half went for food. There were several Englishmen in the factory, who told me the poor creatures were wretchedly fed, and seldom remained more than a year in the establishment.

The population of the villages through which we passed looked very, *very* poor. The houses, which were all of wood, were generally in bad repair, and one or two of them which I looked into contained little or no furniture. We visited the town of Narva, and went first to the old fortress called Ivan Gorod, after John the Terrible, who built it to the no small dismay of the Swedes. The only remarkable thing inside the walls is a church containing an image, said to be miraculous, and a very small round chapel, which traditionally was erected for John the Terrible in twenty-four hours, but which is no longer used as a place of worship. After the fortress we visited Peter the Great's house, which is left in the same state as when he slept there for one night. We were shown a pair of shoes made by him, a thick walking-stick with which he used to belabour his courtiers, a deed with his signature, and the model of a boat he made. The Emperor Nicholas, during his visits to Narva, never inhabited that palace, but lived in a house next door. The Cathedral, which was formerly a Roman Catholic one, differs in shape from the Greek churches, and contains some curious old tombs much defaced. At the Hotel de Ville we saw some curious documents, signed by Charles XII., and then leaving Narva we drove to Tola, about two miles on the opposite side of the river, which is wide, and from whence there was a fine sunset, lighting up the town, which looked picturesque.

St. Petersburg, July 14, 1850.—The sad intelligence of Sir Robert Peel's death reached us by a telegraphic despatch at the same time as the news of his accident, and deeply indeed did we mourn the loss of so great and good a man, and felt that England had been deprived of one of her greatest statesmen, and the Queen of a most valuable and devoted servant and subject. All parties, however much they may have differed from Sir Robert politically, united in expressing appreciation of his character; and on hearing the sad news of his death, the Emperor Nicholas immediately wrote himself to Lady Peel, to express his condolence and the personal regard and respect he had for Sir Robert. The Queen was very much distressed at his loss, and wrote me a touching letter on that occasion.

St. Petersburg, March 4, 1850.—A policeman was accosted here one day by a little boy of five years old, who stated that he was an officer's son, who had died, leaving his widow in great poverty and distress. She also died shortly after giving birth to a second boy, no one being with her at the time but her eldest child, who, not knowing what to do with the infant, wrapped it up in an old shawl, and carried it to a kennel in the yard to a dog who had had puppies, whilst he went to get assistance. The policeman desired to be taken to the spot immediately, where, sure enough, he found the new-born babe lying among the puppies, and sucking their mother. The little boy's story was verified, and the Emperor Nicholas having been informed of these curious facts, adopted the orphans. The eldest was sent to the Corps des Cadets, and the youngest to the Foundling Hospital, to be nursed. This story was related to me by Count Wilihorsky, one of the managers of the hospital, who had just heard it from the Czar.

St. Petersburg, November 26, 1850.—To my great relief and surprise, Lord Bloomfield walked into my room to inform me that he had just had an interview with Count Nesselrode, who told him that Baron Brunnow announced that the Queen having been graciously pleased to request Lord Palmerston to give us another post less trying to my health, we were to be removed from St. Petersburg. We had not yet heard ourselves from Lord Palmerston, and were naturally anxious to know where we were to be sent; but Count Nesselrode said Sir Hamilton Seymour was named as Lord Bloomfield's successor, and shortly after we heard my husband was to succeed Lord Westmoreland at Berlin, who was sent to Vienna. We left St. Petersburg the following spring.

In the summer of 1850, when we were living at the Forestier's, we were just starting one lovely evening for a row on the Neva, when a carriage drove up with two ladies in it, who turned out to be Princess R. and her cousin —— ——. The latter, a charming Pole, had but lately arrived at St. Petersburg, having been ordered to come there for political reasons. She was living at Paris when one day the Russian Chargé d'Affaires walked into her room, and to her great surprise and consternation informed her she was to go to St. Petersburg instantly. She happened to be in delicate health, and quite unfit to travel in the middle of winter, so with some difficulty she was allowed to postpone her departure till the navigation opened, and then she arrived, having never been in Russia before. The first visit she paid was to a countrywoman of her own, who exclaimed, 'Good heavens! what are you doing here? are they going to send you to Siberia?' This was not promising, and she begged in vain to be brought face to face with her accusers, or to be told what she had done. She was merely told she must remain at St. Petersburg, or run the risk of having all her property confiscated. One day we were all invited to a party at the Islands to visit a gipsy camp and hear their music. —— —— arrived, looking as pale as death, so I went up to her and inquired whether she was ill. She said no, only worried, and could she speak a few words to me privately, so we drove together to the gipsy camp, and then she informed me she had heard that her only son, a boy of seven or eight years old, was dangerously ill at Vienna, that she had applied that morning for leave to go to see him, but had been refused, and that she was so unhappy she knew not what to do. I did my best to comfort her, and from that time we became very intimate, and I saw a great deal of her. She was kept about six months at St. Petersburg, whilst her papers were being examined; at the end of that time the head of the police told her that as there was no proof against her, she was at liberty to depart; so to her intense delight she was able to return to her family.

I knew the head of the Secret Police very

well, and he told me one day he had a report every day of what went on in our house, that he knew everyone who went in or out; so I laughed and said he was quite welcome to know all that happened as far as *I* was concerned, as he could not send *me* off to Siberia. He then made me a speech I shall never forget, saying, 'Do you suppose it would be necessary I should *speak* to take away a person's character, not at all. If there was a question of that person in society, and that I shrugged my shoulders and seemed as if they were suspected, "cette personne seroit perdue."'

It frequently happened that people were arrested in the night, and sent off without trial; and one lady who was living in an hotel received notice that she had better be on her guard as to what she said or did in her room, as she was watched. The walls of her room looked all right, but on tapping them she found one place hollow, and on further examination she discovered that the winter supply of wood was piled up in the yard of the hotel against the wall of her room. In that there was a space where a man could watch everything that went on in the room without the occupant being the least aware of the fact.

Another story of a friend of mine was a very remarkable one. She was married at sixteen, and lived in an old castle in Poland, where she gave birth to a son, but after her confinement she was paralysed, and lost the use of her legs. Her husband left her, and led a very wild life at St. Petersburg, and he persuaded her to sign away her property, which he squandered and mortgaged twice over. After some years she became aware of his treachery, and this had such an effect upon her that she fell into very bad health, and had to undergo several terrible operations. She was twice branded with hot irons without chloroform, which in those days had not been discovered, and she was subject to cataleptic attacks, during which she was in a state of *clairvoyance*, and in one of them she became aware of a conspiracy against the Emperor Nicholas' life, and she wrote to the Emperor and gave him information, which gave him a very kindly feeling towards her. During her illness a neighbour arrived on a visit, bringing a clever doctor with him. He saw —— and insisted upon her seeing a very celebrated surgeon from Warsaw, who was the means of saving her life. After this Dr. —— persuaded her to leave Poland and go to Constantinople, where she resided for some time, and made the acquaintance of the captain of an English frigate. She afterwards went to Greece, and there her faithful attendant was taken ill of fever. She, still paralysed, heard his moans in the room next her own, but was unable to go to him; and they were so poor they had scarcely any food in the house, when fortunately Captain ——'s ship arrived at the Piræus, and he, hearing she was at Athens, went to call upon her. He found her in the most helpless condition, not daring to consult a Greek doctor, her own medical man having especially enjoined that whatever happened she was never to trust a Greek physician, so Captain —— brought the ship's doctor to the invalid, and supplied —— with the necessaries of life.

When I made her acquaintance at St. Petersburg she had come there to try and recover her property, and the case was tried in thirteen different courts, which all gave it against her, but the Emperor was the final appeal, and he reversed the sentence of all the courts, and by a stroke of his pen gave her back her estate. Many years after I met her again at Vienna; she had then recovered the use of her limbs, and was very flourishing. It was just at the beginning of the Franco-German war, before the battle of Wörth. We were discussing the probable results of the war, and she said to me, 'Oh, you may be sure the French will be beaten, and Paris will be burnt.' I answered,

'What makes you say that? I think it just as likely the Prussians will be beaten.' 'Oh, no,' she said, 'have you not seen the famous prophecy?' I said, 'No; what prophecy?' so she said, 'Why, the prophecy of Orval, which I read many years ago, and have just seen again at Rome.' She then informed me that during the French Revolution some Poles were travelling, and came to a monastery, where they first heard of the execution of Louis XVI. An old monk further told them that the queen would be executed also, and when they asked him what made him say so, he answered that he was the librarian of the monastery, and had found an ancient prophecy of the fifteenth century, which foretold all the principal events which had happened since, among others the French Revolution.

I myself have since seen the prophecy, which certainly foretold the Wars of Napoleon, the Restoration, the Revolution of '30, when the Fleur de Lys gave place to the Gallican cock, and a king was elected by the people, &c. The prophecy went on to say that after many wars there would be fifteen years of great peace and prosperity, but these would be succeeded by terrible wars, and all further vision was impeded by a wall of fire which the writer believed was the end of the world. An old Roman Catholic bishop I knew at Vienna assured me he himself had read the prophecy at least sixty years ago when he was a boy at school, and before some of the events I have described had occurred.

A friend of mine, Countess S—— D——, told me the following curious story, which was corroborated by her husband. When she was engaged to be married, she was invited, without her betrothed, to a ball at the Grand Duchess Marie's at the Palais Leuchtenberg. Shortly after her arrival she was overpowered by sleep, and quite unable to keep her eyes open she withdrew to a corridor, where she fell fast asleep on a settee. She slept so sound that, though all the company had to pass by her going in to supper, she never awoke, and the Grand Duchess, thinking she was very tired, desired she might not be disturbed, so she slept on till about 3 A.M., when the ball being over she returned home with her mother. When she arrived at her own door she found P—— D—— ready to hand her out of the carriage, and he inquired how she had liked the ball, and whether she had had a good sleep? She was much astonished, and answered that she had been sound asleep most of the time, but asked how he knew it? So he smiled, and said that he had *willed* it, to *dédommager* himself for not having been invited to the ball, which omission had annoyed him very much. He was of a very jealous disposition—the marriage was not a happy one, and ended in a separation; but when I knew them they were living together, and both assured me that the fact I have just related was perfectly true.

Count and Countess M—— were living in the S—— house on the great quay at St. Petersburg, but as they were not rich they only had an apartment there, and the door of the Countess's boudoir was walled off from the rest of the house, but communicated with the drawing-room. One night when the Count and Countess were sitting together they saw the figure of a *chasseur* pass through the drawing-room into the boudoir. They were rather surprised, and the Countess asked her husband to go and see what the man wanted in her boudoir, so the Count got up, and when he went into the boudoir he saw the same figure, which disappeared behind the *portière* of the door, which was walled up. He looked behind the *portière*, but the figure had disappeared, and they saw it no more. Some days after the Count went to dine with the Grand Duchess Helen, and there he met an old friend, the Grand Duchess's brother, Prince Alexander of Wurtemberg. They shook hands, and the Prince expressed great pleasure at meeting him again, asked after the Countess, who had lately married, and inquired where they were living, as he wished to call upon her. Count M—— said they had an apartment in the S—— house, upon which the Prince remarked he had not been there for some years, and that the last time it had been on a painful occasion, as he was called upon to identify the body of a Polish *chasseur*, who had hung himself over a door-way. My dear husband perfectly recollected the fact, which occurred soon after he went to St. Petersburg, but the Count and Countess were *not* aware of it when they saw the apparition.

There was a singular tradition in the B——'s family, that whenever any member of that family broke a looking-glass it was a sure sign of a death. My friend, Countess B——, who was a very sensible, clever woman, told me she could not of course associate the two things, but the fact was undeniable, and she instanced several times in her own married life when the coincidence occurred. One day, Count B—— had gone on a shooting expedition with his friend, Mr. Arthur Magenis, who at that time was Secretary of

Embassy at St. Petersburg ; they had travelled a considerable distance to the place where they were to shoot, and arrived there late in the evening. The following morning, whilst he was shaving, Count B—— knocked down the little looking-glass belonging to his dressing-box, and broke it. He was much alarmed and annoyed, and told his friend he was very sorry to disappoint him, but he felt convinced some misfortune had happened at home, and he must return at once. Mr. Magenis tried to convince him it was all superstitution and nonsense. Count B—— persisted in his resolution, and returned at once to St. Petersburg. He drove straight to his house there, and inquired whether all was well. The answer was that nothing had occurred, but the family were at that time living in the Islands, so Count B—— drove out there at once, and when he arrived he found his mother had died that morning of apoplexy, and they were in the act of laying out the body.

At another time, after the death of her only brother, Countess B—— was looking over his things, and among others there was a very fine English dressing-case. She and Count B—— were looking at it, when the lid fell down with considerable violence. They looked at each other in alarm, and said they hoped nothing was broken, but found on re-opening the box that the looking-glass was shivered to atoms. That very day Prince G——, the Count's brother-in-law, was shot dead coming out of his office in St. Petersburg. Countess B—— told me one or two more instances which had happened to herself, which, unfortunately, I did not write down at the time, and have forgotten.

On one occasion Mr. N—— went to stay with Mr., now Sir A. Buchanan, in the country, where the latter was Secretary of Legation. He showed Mr. N—— various kinds of baths for washing purposes, and asked which he would like to have in his room. Mr. N—— smiled, but said he had quite given up washing, as he was sure it was a very dangerous habit. That having been educated in England he was always accustomed to using a tub; but he found all his cotemporaries died, and as he was sure it was owing to their tubbing so much, he had quite given up that bad habit, and now only had a bath occasionally, 'pour raisons de propreté!'

In the winter of 1850 I was invited to a great ball at the Grand Duke Héritier's at the Winter Palace at St. Petersburg. I was sitting at the end of the ball-room, a magnificent long gallery, on a sofa with Pauline Bartenieff, one of the maids-of-honour, when the Empress came up to us and took her place beside me, where Her Imperial Majesty remained a considerable time. When she rose she turned round to me and said, 'Suivez-moi,' which I did for some time; but people evidently wondered why I was in close attendance on the Empress, and what business I had to follow her about, so after a time I got annoyed, and returned to my seat. Presently there was a great hubbub in the crowd, and various chamberlains hurried to and fro asking for me; at last one came up and said the Empress wanted me.

I immediately got up and followed him to where Her Majesty was standing, upon which she playfully struck me with her fan saying, 'Méchante, pourquoi m'avez-vous abandonnée: ne vous avais-je pas dit de me suivre?' I tried to explain that I thought I had done so long enough, and was unwilling to appear intrusive, but the Empress would listen to no excuse, but said, 'Non, non, suivez-moi.' After a time we reached the middle of the gallery, where the Cotillon was being danced, then the Empress to my extreme astonishment sent for two chairs, sat upon one herself, and ordered me to sit on the other! The surprise of the by-standers was undisguised, and I could not myself account for this sudden expression of Imperial favour, except by supposing it was a freak of the Empress's to gratify my intimate friend, the Countess Sophie Bobrinsky, who was a great favourite with the Empress. I was amused some time after on paying a visit to Princess G——, who spoke to me about her anxiety to get one of her daughters appointed a maid-of-honour, at her saying in answer to my observation that I did not imagine it would be very difficult, 'Pas pour vous, Madame, qui êtes tellement favorisée à la Cour que tout doit vous être facile ; mais pour moi, un humble individu, une telle grâce n'est pas probable !'

In Russia, where a smile or a nod from any member of the Imperial family was valued beyond all belief, such a proof of favour as I had received made a tremendous sensation, but, as far as *I* was concerned, 'c'en est resté là.'

The balls at the Winter Palace were by far the finest I ever saw anywhere. The splendour of the uniforms, jewels, and dresses was quite unique, and the rooms were so brilliantly lighted ! One day I asked out of curiosity how many candles were used for one *fête*, and was told the number was about 36,000, which I can quite believe, as all the immense rooms were lighted with candles—there was no gas. The supper tables were gorgeous, and so constructed as to admit large orange-trees, covered with golden fruit, at distances which gave a most fairy-like appearance to the whole scene.

The other day Dr. Gutzlaff, the famous Chinese missionary, dined with us, and his conversation was extremely interesting and amusing. He lived twenty-three years in China, and looked exactly like a Chinese. He had a dry but very comical way of relating stories, which amused us exceedingly, and his report of the progress of Christianity in China was deeply interesting. Since 1844, when liberty of conscience was first allowed, the number of converts seems to have increased rapidly, and now it appears that places of Christian worship have been established throughout the land. There are a vast number of missionaries among the Chinese themselves, and though they need much instruction, God's blessing seems to attend their simple efforts, and they have done great good. Dr. Gutzlaff came to Europe for the sake of enlisting the sympathy of his Christian brethren in behalf of the Chinese, and told me he hoped he had secured the services of fifty men and ten women, who were ready to go to China to instruct the native missionaries.

We went to a *fête* at Count Kousheleff Bezborodko's, which was one of the prettiest I ever saw. The large garden was entirely lit with coloured lamps, and the borders of a good-sized lake were lighted with lamps in the shape of stars. We proceeded to an island, where there was some pretty music, and then very good fireworks and Bengal lights; the public were admitted to another part of the garden, and the reflection in the waters of such a number of different figures and costumes had a most weird and beautiful effect. The entertainment ended with a ball and supper. The night was perfectly still and very warm, so everything was favourable for the success of the *fête*. The weather was extremely hot, the thermometer constantly above 80° night and day, with occasional terrific thunderstorms, and vivid flashes of lightning, which reminded me of Martin's picture of the Siege of Jerusalem!

The last winter we spent in Russia was very severe. For six weeks the thermometer varied between 15 and 30 degrees of frost Réaumur, which is between zero and 30 degrees below zero Fahrenheit.

Captain Robbins, one of the Queen's messengers, arrived, having made a perilous journey.

The weather was so bad that before he reached Warsaw, his fellow-traveller refused to go on. Captain Robbins declared he would not stop till he was obliged, and started in his britzka. The cold was so intense he fell asleep, and woke to find his carriage upset in a ditch, the postillion and horses gone, and the window smashed. The night was dark and stormy, the snow falling heavily, and he heard wolves howling, so he kept firing off pistols during the night; and early the next morning his friend, who was following him to Warsaw, arrived, saw the head of the carriage above the snow, and wondered what had become of Robbins, who was extricated from his perilous position and came on to St. Petersburg; but when he arrived his travelling cap was frozen to his head and he was so petrified with cold that he was some days recovering. There were no rail-roads in Russia when I left it in 1851, and travelling in winter was very difficult, and still more so at the break-up of the ice in the spring; for the rivers had then to be passed in ferry-boats, and these were often smashed by the ice coming down. The snow, too, instead of being smooth and pleasant for sledging, got into what the Russians called 'uchabs,' or like ridge and furrow, so that the motion was extremely disagreeable, like the rocking of a boat at sea, and the immense tracts of flat country, without a tree or a house, were dreary in the extreme.

The following story was told me on December 25, 1850, by Princess L—— as having happened to her maternal great grandfather :—

In the year 17— Count R——, a Polish nobleman, between forty and fifty years of age, went to Cracow for the Carnival. He was there invited to a large dinner party of gentlemen, many of whom were old friends whom he had not met for many years. After dinner the cup went merrily round, the guests partook of it very freely, and several stories were related ; among others, one was told by Count R——, when in a state of intoxication, which was so very dreadful many of the guests left the room. When the Count became sober his friends told him what he had revealed, which greatly distressed him, as he had bound himself by a solemn oath never to speak on the painful subject ; but he could not recall his words, and was relieved at hearing he had betrayed no names.

In consequence of what had occurred he made a vow never to touch wine again, which resolution he observed to his dying day ; but he once related the following facts to his grand-daughter, who, in turn, confided them to her daughter, my informant.

When a very young man, Count R—— was living on terms of great intimacy with a family at Cracow, which consisted of a gentleman, his wife, and daughter, a beautiful girl of sixteen. Being suddenly ordered to quit Cracow, the Count went to a great ball to take leave of his friends, who were all three present at it. They quitted the ball-room shortly before him, but when he returned home, having finished all his preparations for his journey, he determined to spend his few remaining hours at his friend's house, and thither he accordingly went. He was surprised to find the entrance-door open, lights burning, but no servants were visible. However, he ascended the principal staircase, passed through a long suite of apartments to the room usually occupied by his friend; but when he entered, he found, to his extreme horror and consternation, his friend standing with a drawn sword on the point of beheading his lovely daughter. Count R—— rushed forward, and arresting his arm, asked him, in God's name, to desist from perpetrating so horrible and atrocious a crime. The other man answered with the utmost calmness that his prayers and entreaties were perfectly useless, that he could not tell him the family mystery which forced him to such an act, but that his child's doom was irrevocably fixed, and that he must insist upon Count R——'s swearing upon the Bible never to reveal what he had accidentally discovered. Count R——, who could not bring himself to believe his senses, had no choice but to take the oath; but on seeing his friend approach the girl to carry the deed into execution he fainted, and when he came to himself no trace of what had occurred remained, and he immediately left Cracow.

Nothing further transpired except that he heard some time after a report that the young lady had been carried off by a sudden attack of illness, but no suspicion rested upon her parents, and every circumstance of that dreadful night seemed buried in oblivion; but in the year 1825 a young Polish nobleman attended by a priest arrived at Cracow, and alighted at one of the principal hotels. On entering the large room which had been assigned to them, the priest showed signs of great agitation. He was interrogated as to the cause of his being so deeply affected, when he declared that many years previously he had nearly witnessed a horrible murder in that very room. At that period he was living in a monastery, where it was customary for one priest to keep watch during the night in case of a sudden summons to a sick person requiring extreme unction. It was his turn to watch, when, being summoned, he found two men in masks waiting for him at the monastery gate, who blindfolded him and pushed him into a carriage. He was driven through the streets for a considerable time, with the evident intention of puzzling him as to the locality, when at last they got out, and he was led up a staircase and through a suite of rooms, till arriving at a boudoir the bandage was removed from his eyes, and he found himself in the presence of a lovely girl and a middle-aged man, apparently her father, who told him he must receive the girl's confession, and immediately after administer extreme unction, as she was about to die, and no mortal power could save her. The young lady herself assured the priest that her doom was irrevocably fixed, so that all intercession would be perfectly useless ; so he fulfilled the duties of his office, but then threw himself at the man's feet and used every argument to dissuade him from this deed of violence. He was, however, silenced, and carried into an adjoining apartment. Presently the gentleman he had seen came towards him, and offered him a glass of wine, which he durst not refuse; but suspecting foul play he did not swallow it, but spat it into his handkerchief, after which he was again blindfolded, and conducted back to his monastery. He at once went to the prior, and told him everything that had occurred. On examining the handkerchief they found it was burnt into holes, evidently from the effects of a most powerful poison, but as they had no clue whatever to the locality where the events narrated had occurred, and the priest having no proof in support of his story, they determined to wait and see whether some circumstance would not transpire which might lead to the discovery of the crime; but after waiting some months in vain, the priest begged to be allowed to leave Cracow, and he was sent to a monastery in a distant part of Poland, after having made a deposition of the above facts, and declaring most solemnly that in her confession the young lady avowed herself perfectly pure and innocent, so that he could not in any way account for the murder. Upon this, most minute inquiries were made as to the former proprietors of the mansion, but nothing was ever discovered as to the perpetrators of the crime, only the priest's story curiously corroborated Count R——'s evidence.

Old Countess R—— was an agreeable old

lady who frequented the *salons* at St. Petersburg, and was always beautifully dressed, though as she was considerably past seventy, the rose-coloured satin she was in the habit of wearing was scarcely suitable. I heard one day that she had lost her brother, and as it is usual in Russia to pay visits of condolence, I hastened to call upon her. I found the rooms darkened, the blinds down, and when I entered her *salon* instead of my brilliant friend I had difficulty in distinguishing a heap of something black in the corner of the room, and a feeble voice greeted me. I suppose I was unable to disguise my astonishment, which was great, when my friend informed me that the Russians consider all ornament superfluous when they are in deep mourning, so they doff their wigs, leave off their rouge and false teeth, and wear a most unbecoming cap, which comes half over their foreheads in a point. In the present instance the change was so remarkable that I literally did not recognise my friend, but I was equally surprised and astonished when about six weeks after she reappeared in society in her pink satin and lace, wig, rouge, and *râtelier*!

Lord Bloomfield having been appointed to Berlin, we left St. Petersburg on May 26, 1851, for Warsaw, where we went that I might take leave of the Emperor and Empress. The road was excellent, and the post-houses we stopped at tolerably clean, as they had been prepared for the Empress, who had preceded us a few days previously. Every house had been whitewashed, and every post repainted, but beyond clean rooms and a leather sofa, we found but little accommodation, and travellers were obliged to take all they required with them. The distance between the two capitals is 1,057 versts. We slept at Katejnoi, Régitsa, Ouziany, Marianpol, and Lomza. In Russia, when persons of distinction travelled they got an official order, called a padorojni, for horses and admittance into the best rooms at the post-houses, and when we reached Lomza we were informed rooms had been ordered for us at the Government House. We were accordingly shown into an enormous apartment, which had been occupied by the Empress, but which was nevertheless full of bugs, and the slops had never been emptied, so the rooms were anything but odoriferous. At Marianpol I found the post-house so cold I begged to have the stove lighted, which was done, but my French maid did not see that the damper was closed, so I was very nearly asphyxiated with the fumes of the charcoal. I woke feeling very queer, and with a most violent headache, but as I luckily discovered the cause of my discomfort I opened the window, and the fresh air soon restored me. The Louga, Dwina, Niemen, and Vistula are all fine large rivers, but the country we travelled through was perfectly flat and uninteresting, and nothing could be more monotonous than the road—boundless plains, very thinly populated and badly cultivated, only occasionally varied by fir-forests. There was, however, a marked difference in the vegetation as we approached Warsaw. When we left St. Petersburg the leaves of the lilacs and birches were only budding, whereas at Vilkomir, which we passed on the third day, the lilacs and horse-chestnuts were already in full flower.

The weather was wet and cold, and the only place the least picturesque was Kowno, formerly the frontier town between Russia and Poland. Now the Russians have endeavoured to destroy all trace of the frontier, the Russian colours are painted everywhere, and Kowno seemed entirely peopled by Jews—a dirtier, more disgusting population I never beheld ; but the women looked picturesque, and wore a kind of turban, and the men wore long beards, in spite of their being forbidden under a heavy penalty. Nearly all the business in the villages in Poland was in the hands of the Jews, and it was curious to see the cottages nearly one and all lighted up on the Sabbath eve when, as the Messiah is expected, the men go to the synagogue, and the women stay at home baking unleavened bread. At Ostrolenka, where the last great battle was fought between the Poles and the Russians in 1831, a gaudy Imperial monument had been raised in memory of the Russians who fell there, whilst a few wooden crosses marked the graves of the poor Poles, very emblematic of the condition of the two countries. The evening was beautiful as we approached Warsaw, and the lights and shadows on the palaces and churches very fine, as they rose up above the Vistula.

Sunday, June 8.—After divine service at the English chapel, which was performed in one of the old palaces, we walked in the Saxon garden, so called from its having belonged to a palace where the Electors of Saxony, who wished to become Kings of Poland, resided.

On Monday we received an invitation to dine with the Emperor and Empress at Lazincki, the palace which formerly belonged to Poniatowski, and which is exceedingly pretty—not large, but the rooms well proportioned, and where there were some fine pictures. There we met at dinner General Prince Windischgrätz, General Hess, and Prince François Lichtenstein, and their respective suites. The Emperor Nicholas wore the Austrian uniform, out of compliment to them, but with his usual *galanterie* apologised to us for receiving us in that costume. Marshal Prince Paskéwitch and a number of Russian swere at dinner; but no Poles, except Prince and Princess Léon Radziwill and Count Krasinsky. The rule established at St. Petersburg of receiving no Poles except those who are in the Russian service was also strictly observed at Warsaw, the consequence being that scarcely any of the Polish nobility went to Court, and most of them strictly avoided it. As nothing was done to conciliate them, they made no secret of their dislike of the Russians, and kept as much aloof from them as possible.

On Tuesday, my husband attended a parade, and in the evening we were invited to a ballet in the theatre at Lazincki, which was elegantly fitted up, but to my great disappointment instead of seeing something national there was a stupid ballet called the 'Bandit's Daughter.'

On Wednesday morning the Empress sent for me at eleven o'clock, and kept me an hour and a half. She was most kind in her expressions of regret at our leaving Russia, and at having had so few opportunities of seeing me during my residence at St. Petersburg.

Certainly but little civility and attention was shown to the Corps Diplomatique as a body there, and though all the members of the Imperial family were kind and gracious when we did meet them, the opportunities of doing so were few and far between. Just as I was leaving the Emperor came in from a parade, and I took leave of him, and never saw him again.

We dined at Count Auguste Potocki's country seat, Willany, the finest place in the vicinity of Warsaw, one might almost say, in Poland; for it is one of the very few properties which has never been confiscated, and abounds in interesting pictures and historical souvenirs. It was built by Jean Sobieski after his return from Vienna, and one wing of the house remains exactly as it was in his day. The gardens were well kept and the trees very fine. I was particularly struck by one black poplar, which five men could not reach round; and the difference in the growth and appearance of vegetation in Poland to what it is at St. Petersburg was very remarkable—everything there looks so stunted and poor. There is a hospital for sixty patients at Willany, schools, and altogether it is a fine establishment. Countess Potocki had unfortunately left home, but Count Auguste received us most kindly, showed us all over the place, and gave us a very good dinner. On our return home we visited the fine church of St. Croix. In the crypt below we saw the body of a monk lying in his coffin surrounded with tapers, and the vaults of the Czartoryskis and Lubomirskis, which were well aired, and the coffins were bricked in, so there was scarcely any disagreeable smell in this last resting-place of the distinguished dead. On June 5 I left Warsaw for Breslau. I arrived at Berlin on the 8th, having travelled through a flat and most uninteresting country, but a remarkable difference was observable in the villages and cultivation as soon as we reached the Prussian frontier. There was a much greater appearance of wealth, civilisation, and cleanliness—the peasants were much better clad; and altogether I had the feeling of being once more in Europe.

END OF THE FIRST VOLUME.

LONDON: PRINTED BY
SPOTTISWOODE AND CO., NEW-STREET SQUARE
AND PARLIAMENT STREET

www.ingramcontent.com/pod-product-compliance
Lightning Source LLC
Chambersburg PA
CBHW021104270326
41929CB00009B/733
9783337094843